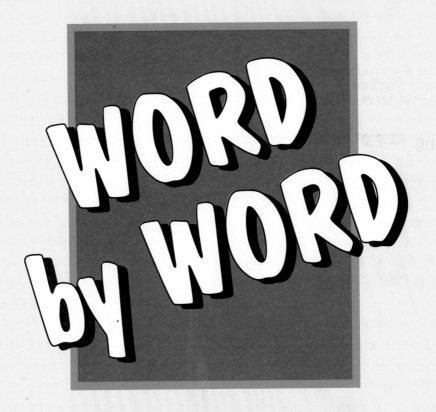

WORD by WORD

Dicionário Ilustrado de Inglês

English/Portuguese Picture Dictionary

Steven J. Molinsky · Bill Bliss

Lynn Mario T. Menezes de Souza

Prentice Hall Regents

Publisher: *Tina B. Carver*
Director of Production: *Aliza Greenblatt*
Managing editor, production: *Dominick Mosco*
Electronic production: *Kelly Tavares, Steven K. Jorgensen*
Interior design: *Kenny Beck*
Cover supervisor: *Marianne Frasco*
Cover design: *Merle Krumper*
Buyer/scheduler: *Ray Keating*

Illustrated by RICHARD E. HILL

Printed in the United States of America

20 19 18 17 16 15 14 13 12 11

ISBN 0-13-128018-X

CONTENTS
CONTEÚDO

O Dicionário Ilustrado *Word by Word* apresenta mais de 3,000 vocábulos através de ilustrações atraentes e coloridas. Este Dicionário Ilustrado inovador oferece ao aprendiz da língua inglesa o vocabulário essencial necessário para se comunicarem com eficácia numa ampla série de situações e contextos.

Em *Word by Word* o vocabulário está organizado em 100 unidades temáticas, oferecendo uma cuidadosa sequência de lições desde o mundo imediato do aprendiz até contextos mais amplos. Unidades iniciais sobre a família, a casa, e atividades cotidianas antecedem lições sobre a comunidade, a escola, o local de trabalho, as compras, as atividades recreativas e outros tópicos. *Word by Word* oferece uma cobertura extensa de vários tópicos imprescindíveis além do vocabulário de matérias escolares e atividades extracurriculares. Dada a autonomia de suas unidades, *Word by Word* pode ser utilizado ou na sequência apresentada ou conforme as necessidades do aprendiz.

Para a conveniência do usuário, as unidades de *Word by Word* aparecem indicadas de duas formas: de maneira sequencial no Conteúdo, e em órdem alfabética no Índice Temático. Esses recursos, juntos com o Glossário no apêndice, permitem que os aprendizes e os professores possam facilmente localizar todas as palavras e os tópicos do Dicionário Ilustrado.

O Dicionário Ilustrado *Word by Word* é o componente principal de todo o Programa de Desenvolvimento de Vocabulário *Word by Word*, que consiste de uma grande seleção de materiais de apoio para a aprendizagem da língua inglesa em todos os níveis. Materiais auxiliares incluem workbooks para três níveis diferentes (Alfabetização, Iniciante, e Intermediário), um Manual do Professor (Teacher's Resource Book), um Manual de Estratégias de Ensino de Vocabulário (Handbook of Vocabulary Teaching Strategies), um programa de audio completo, cartazes com ilustrações, transparências coloridas, cartas de jogos de vocabulário, um livro de músicas acompanhado por um songbook, e um programa de avalição e testes. Edições bilingues do Dicionário Ilustrado em várias línguas também estão disponíveis.

Estratégias de Ensino

Word by Word apresenta os ítens de vocabulário sempre de forma contextualizada. Diálogos-modelo exemplificam as situações nas quais as palavras são normalmente utilizadas de forma comunicativa e significativa. Esses diálogos levam o aprendiz a práticas conversacionais interativas e dinâmicas. Além disso, em cada unidade, atividades de escrita e de debate levam os aprendizes a relacionar o vocabulário e os temas a suas próprias vidas na medida em que trocam experiências, opiniões e informações sobre si mesmas, sobre suas culturas, e sobre seus países. Dessa forma os aprendizes chegam a se conhecer «word by word».

Ao usar *Word by Word*, você é estimulado a desenvolver abordagens e estratégias compatíveis com seu próprio estilo de ensinar e com as necessidades e as habilidades de seus alunos. Sugerimos as seguintes técnicas para a apresentação e prática do vocabulário de cada unidade.

1. *Atividades preparatórias para a Apresentação do Vocabulário:* Procure ativar o conhecimento prévio dos alunos discutindo com eles as palavras que já conhecem na unidade, escrevendo-as na lousa ou mostrando aos alunos os cartazes (Wall Chart), as transparências ou as ilustrações no livro, fazendo com que identifiquem as palavras já conhecidas.

2. *Atividades de Apresentação do Vocabulário:* Aponte para a ilustração de cada palavra, diga a palavra, e peça aos alunos que a repitam juntos e individualmente. Verifique a compreensão e pronúncia dos alunos com relação a cada ítem do vocabulário.

3. *Atividades de Prática:* Os alunos podem praticar o vocabulário juntos, em pares, ou em grupos pequenos. Diga ou escreva uma palavra e peça aos alunos que apontem para o ítem ou que digam o número do ítem. Outra possibilidade é apontar para o ítem ou dizer o número de um determinado ítem, e pedir aos alunos que digam a palavra.

4. *Atividades de Prática com os Diálogos-Modelo:* Algumas unidades possuem diálogos-modelo que utilizam o primeiro ítem na lista de vocabulário. Outros

diálogos-modelo têm uma forma apenas esqueletal, na qual os ítens de vocabulário possam ser inseridas. (Em muitos diálogos desse tipo há números que indicam quais das palavras podem ser utilizadas para completar o diálogo. Nos casos em que não há nenhum número, todas as palavras na página podem ser utilizadas.)

a. Atividade Preparatória: Os alunos examinam os diálogos-modelo e procuram identificar os participantes e o contexto do diálogo.

b. O professor apresenta o modelo e verifica a compreensão dos alunos quanto ao contexto e o vocabulário.

c. Os alunos repetem juntos ou individualmente, cada linha do diálogo.

d. Os alunos praticam o diálogo em pares.

e. Um par de alunos apresenta um diálogo novo baseado no diálogo modelo, utilizando uma palavra diferente da lista de vocabulário.

f. Em pares, os alunos praticam vários diálogos novos baseados no diálogo modelo utilizando ítens diferentes do vocabulário.

g. Os pares apresentam seus diálogos para a classe toda.

5. *Atividades adicionais de Prática Conversacional:* Várias das unidades oferecem dois diálogos esqueletais adicionais para práticas conversacionais suplementares com o vocabulário. (Essas são indicadas pela cor amarela no rodapé da página.) Os alunos podem praticar e apresentar esses diálogos, utilizando as palavras que quiserem.

6. *Atividades de Prática Ortográfica e de Escrita:* Os alunos podem praticar soletrando as palavras em conjunto, em pares ou em pequenos grupos. Diga ou soletre uma palavra e peça aos alunos que a escrevam e a indiquem nas ilustrações ou que digam o número da palavra. Ou então, aponte para a ilustração de um item ou dê seu número e peça aos alunos que escrevam a palavra.

7. *Temas para Debates, Redações, Diários e Arquivos:* Cada unidade de *Word by Word* oferece uma ou mais questões para debates e redações. (Essas questões são indicadas pela cor verde no rodapé da página.) Os alunos podem responder às questões em conjunto, em pares ou em pequenos grupos. Ou então, os alunos podem escrever suas respostas em casa, trocar suas respostas escritas com outros alunos e discutir as questões em conjunto, em pares ou em pequenos grupos.

Os alunos poderão gostar de manter um diário com seus trabalhos escritos. Caso haja tempo, você poderá querer escrever uma resposta sua em cada diário dos alunos, trocando com eles suas próprias opiniões e experiências, além de reagir àquilo que o aluno tem escrito. Caso você mantenha um arquivo dos trabalhos escritos de seus alunos, os mesmos servem como exemplos excelentes do progresso dos alunos na aprendizagem da língua inglesa.

8. *Atividades Comunicativas:* O Manual do Professor de *Word by Word* oferece uma grande quantidade de jogos, atividades, tarefas, debates, movimentos, desenhos, mímicas, dramatizações e outras atividades, cujo objetivo é maximizar os estilos de aprendizagem e as habilidades diferentes dos alunos. Para cada unidade, escolha uma ou mais das atividades para reforçar a aprendizagem do vocabulário de uma maneira estimulante, criativa e divertida.

Word by Word visa oferecer aos alunos uma maneira comunicativa, significativa e dinâmica de praticar o vocabulário da língua inglesa. Ao oferecer essas explicações sobre a substância de nosso programa, esperamos ter também comunicado o espírito por trás do mesmo: que a aprendizagem de vocabulário pode ser verdadeiramente interativa ... relevante à vida dos alunos ... atenta a seus diferentes estilos de aprendizagem e habilidades ... e divertida!

Steven J. Molinsky
Bill Bliss

The *Word by Word* Picture Dictionary presents more than 3,000 vocabulary words through lively full-color illustrations. This innovative Picture Dictionary offers students the essential vocabulary they need to communicate effectively in a wide range of relevant situations and contexts.

Word by Word organizes the vocabulary into 100 thematic units, providing a careful sequence of lessons that range from the immediate world of the student to the world at large. Early units on the family, the home, and daily activities lead to lessons on the community, school, workplace, shopping, recreation, and other topics. *Word by Word* offers extensive coverage of important lifeskill competencies and the vocabulary of school subjects and extracurricular activities. Since each unit is self-contained, *Word by Word* can be used either sequentially or in any desired order.

For users' convenience, the units in *Word by Word* are listed two ways: sequentially in the Table of Contents, and alphabetically in the Thematic Index. These resources, combined with the Glossary in the appendix, allow students and teachers to quickly and easily locate all words and topics in the Picture Dictionary.

The *Word by Word* Picture Dictionary is the centerpiece of the complete *Word by Word* Vocabulary Development Program, which offers a wide selection of print and media support materials for instruction at all levels. Ancillary materials include Workbooks at three different levels (Literacy, Beginning, and Intermediate), a Teacher's Resource Book, a Handbook of Vocabulary Teaching Strategies, a complete Audio Program, Wall Charts, Color Transparencies, Vocabulary Game Cards, a Song Album and accompanying Song Book, and a Testing Program. Bilingual editions of the Picture Dictionary are also available.

Teaching Strategies

Word by Word presents vocabulary words in context. Model conversations depict situations in which people use the words in meaningful communication. These models become the basis for students to engage in dynamic, interactive conversational practice. In addition, writing and discussion questions in each unit encourage students to relate the vocabulary and themes to their own lives as they share experiences, thoughts, opinions, and information about themselves, their cultures, and their countries. In this way, students get to know each other "word by word."

In using *Word by Word*, we encourage you to develop approaches and strategies that are compatible with your own teaching style and the needs and abilities of your students. You may find it helpful to incorporate some of the following techniques for presenting and practicing the vocabulary in each unit.

1. *Previewing the Vocabulary:* Activate students' prior knowledge of the vocabulary either by brainstorming with students the words in the unit they already know and writing them on the board, or by having students look at the Wall Chart, the transparency, or the illustration in *Word by Word* and identify the words they are familiar with.

2. *Presenting the Vocabulary:* Point to the picture of each word, say the word, and have the class repeat it chorally and individually. Check students' understanding and pronunciation of the vocabulary.

3. *Vocabulary Practice:* Have students practice the vocabulary as a class, in pairs, or in small groups. Say or write a word, and have students point to the item or tell the number. Or, point to an item or give the number, and have students say the word.

4. *Model Conversation Practice:* Some units have model conversations that use the first word in the vocabulary list. Other models

are in the form of *skeletal dialogs*, in which vocabulary words can be inserted. (In many skeletal dialogs, bracketed numbers indicate which words can be used to practice the conversation. If no bracketed numbers appear, all the words on the page can be used.)

The following steps are recommended for Model Conversation Practice:

a. Preview: Students look at the model illustration and discuss who they think the speakers are and where the conversation takes place.

b. The teacher presents the model and checks students' understanding of the situation and the vocabulary.

c. Students repeat each line of the conversation chorally or individually.

d. Students practice the model in pairs.

e. A pair of students presents a new conversation based on the model, but using a different word from the vocabulary list.

f. In pairs, students practice several new conversations based on the model, using different vocabulary words.

g. Pairs present their conversations to the class.

5. *Additional Conversation Practice:* Many units provide two additional skeletal dialogs for further conversation practice with the vocabulary. (These can be found in a yellow-shaded area at the bottom of the page.) Have students practice and present these conversations using any words they wish.

6. *Writing and Spelling Practice:* Have students practice spelling the words as a class, in pairs, or in small groups. Say or spell a word, and have students write it and then point to the picture of the item or tell the number. Or, point to a picture of an item or give the number, and have students write the word.

7. *Themes for Discussion, Composition, Journals, and Portfolios:* Each unit of *Word by Word* provides one or more questions for discussion and composition. (These can be found in a green-shaded area at the bottom of the page.) Have students respond to the questions as a class, in pairs, or in small groups. Or, have students write their responses at home, share their written work with other students, and discuss as a class, in pairs, or in small groups.

Students may enjoy keeping a journal of their written work. If time permits, you may want to write a response in each student's journal, sharing your own opinions and experiences as well as reacting to what the student has written. If you are keeping portfolios of students' work, these compositions serve as excellent examples of students' progress in learning English.

8. *Communication Activities:* The *Word by Word* Teacher's Resource Book provides a wealth of games, tasks, brainstorming, discussion, movement, drawing, miming, role-playing, and other activities designed to take advantage of students' different learning styles and particular abilities and strengths. For each unit, choose one or more of these activities to reinforce students' vocabulary learning in a way that is stimulating, creative, and enjoyable.

Word by Word aims to offer students a communicative, meaningful, and lively way of practicing English vocabulary. In conveying to you the substance of our program, we hope that we have also conveyed the spirit: that learning vocabulary can be genuinely interactive . . . relevant to our students' lives . . . responsive to students' differing strengths and learning styles . . . and fun!

Steven J. Molinsky
Bill Bliss

A. What's your **name**?
B. *Nancy Ann Peterson.*

nome completo	**1.** name	
nome	**2.** first name	
outro(s) nome(s)	**3.** middle name	
sobrenome	**4.** last name/family name/ surname	
endereço	**5.** address	
número	**6.** street number	
rua	**7.** street	
apartamento	**8.** apartment number	
cidade	**9.** city	
estado	**10.** state	
código postal	**11.** zip code	
código telefónico	**12.** area code	
número de telefone	**13.** telephone number/ phone number	
número de previdência social	**14.** social security number	

A. What's your _____?
B. ....
A. Did you say ....?
B. Yes. That's right.

A. What's your last name?
B. ....
A. How do you spell that?
B. ....

Tell about yourself:
  My name is ....
  My address is ....
  My telephone number is ....
Now interview a friend.

A. Who is she?
B. She's my **wife**.
A. What's her name?
B. Her name is *Betty*.

A. Who is he?
B. He's my **husband**.
A. What's his name?
B. His name is *Fred*.

esposa	**1.** wife	irmão	**8.** brother
marido	**2.** husband	bebê, nenê	**9.** baby

pais	**parents**	**avós**	**grandparents**
mãe	**3.** mother	avó	**10.** grandmother
pai	**4.** father	avô	**11.** grandfather

filhos	**children**	**netos**	**grandchildren**
filha	**5.** daughter	neta	**12.** granddaughter
filho	**6.** son	neto	**13.** grandson
irmã	**7.** sister		

A. I'd like to introduce my _____.
B. Nice to meet you.
C. Nice to meet you, too.

A. What's your _____'s name?
B. His/Her name is ....

Tell about your family.
Talk about photos of family members.

A. Who is she?
B. She's my **aunt**.
A. What's her name?
B. Her name is *Linda*.

A. Who is he?
B. He's my **uncle**.
A. What's his name?
B. His name is *Jack*.

tia	**1.** aunt	sogra	**6.** mother-in-law
tio	**2.** uncle	sogro	**7.** father-in-law
sobrinha	**3.** niece	genro	**8.** son-in-law
sobrinho	**4.** nephew	nora	**9.** daughter-in-law
primo, prima	**5.** cousin	cunhado	**10.** brother-in-law
		cunhada	**11.** sister-in-law

A. Is he/she your _____?
B. No. He's/She's my _____.
A. Oh. What's his/her name?
B. ....

A. Let me introduce my _____.
B. I'm glad to meet you.
C. Nice meeting you, too.

Tell about your relatives:
   What are their names?
   Where do they live?
Draw your family tree and talk
   about it.

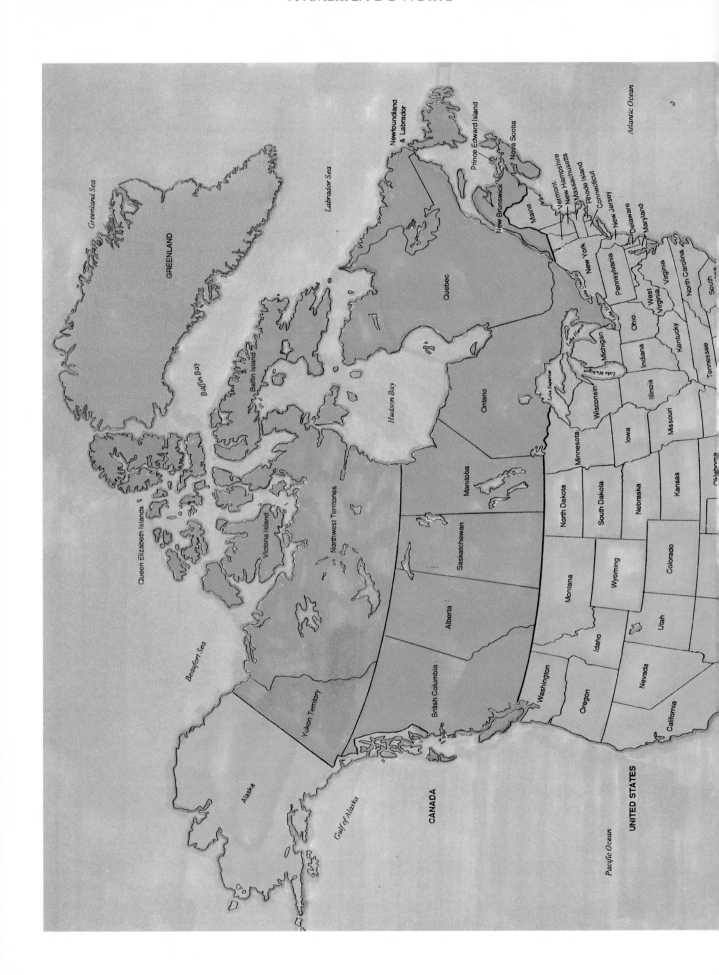

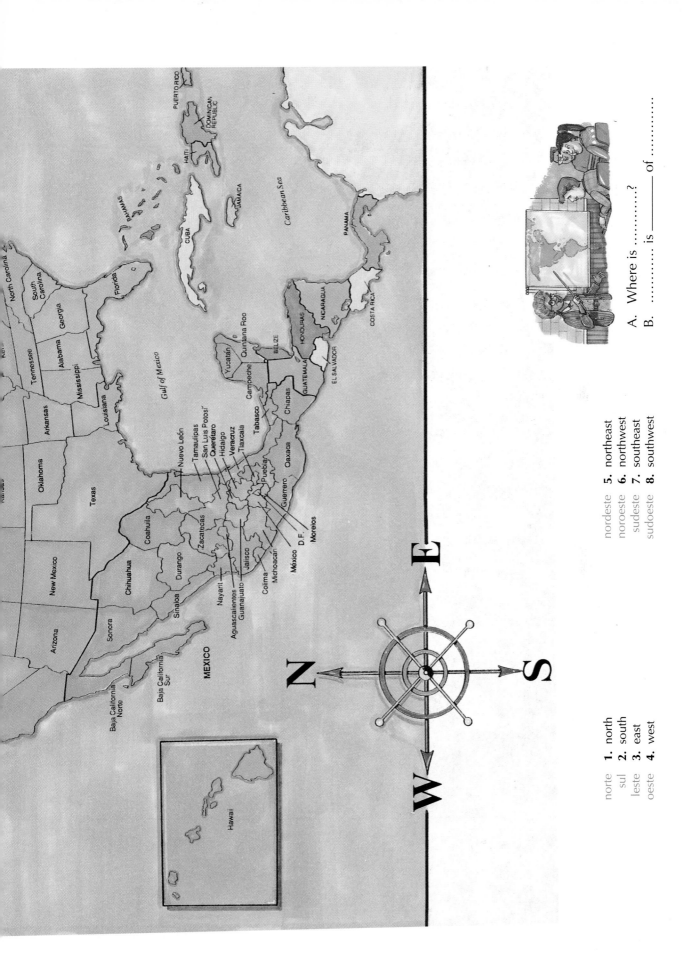

A. Where is ....?

B. .... is —— of ....

norte	1. north	nordeste	5. northeast
sul	2. south	noroeste	6. northwest
leste	3. east	sudeste	7. southeast
oeste	4. west	sudoeste	8. southwest

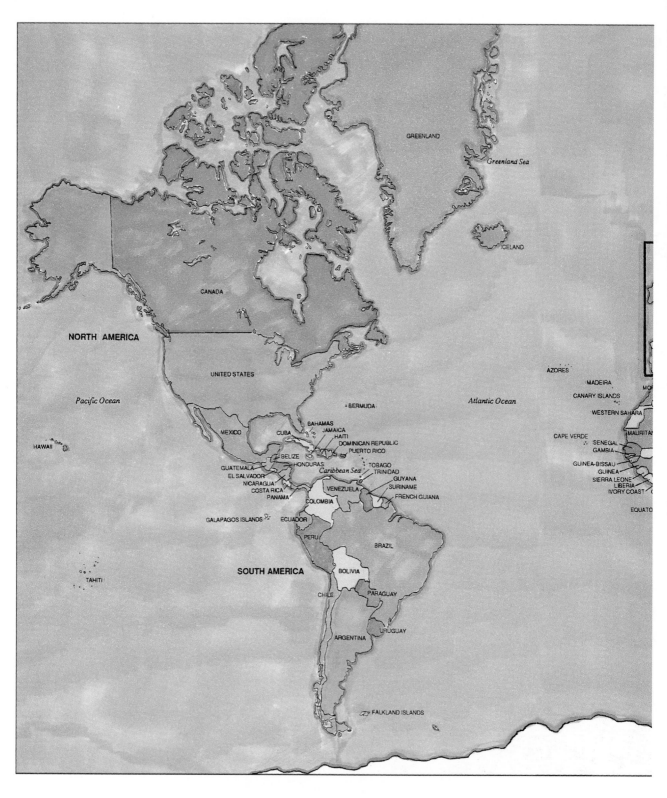

América do Norte	**1.** North America	Oriente Médio	**5.** The Middle East
América do Sul	**2.** South America	Ásia	**6.** Asia
Europa	**3.** Europe	Austrália	**7.** Australia
África	**4.** Africa	Antártica	**8.** Antarctica

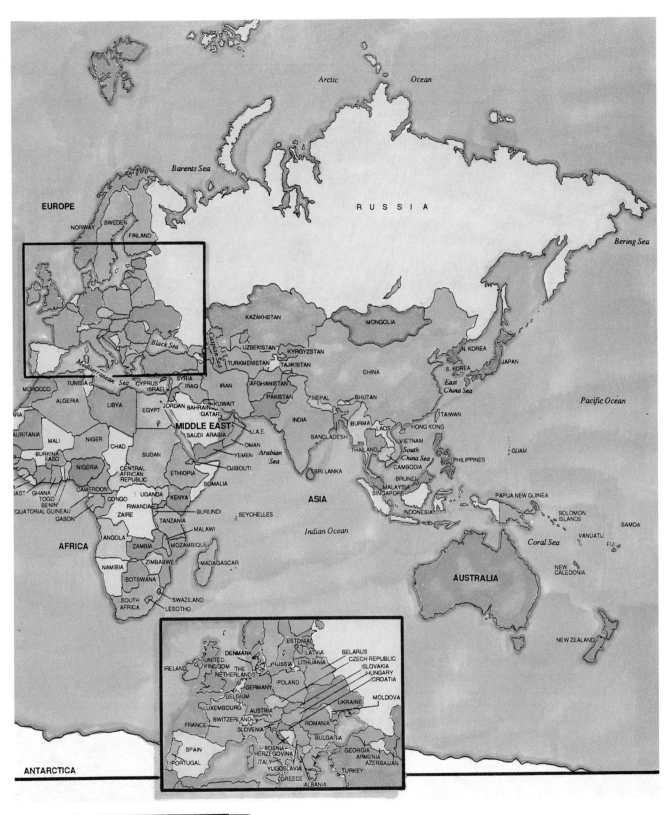

A. Where's ………?   A. What ocean/sea is near
B. It's in _____.   ………?

A. What do you do every day?
B. I **get up**, I **take a shower**, and I **brush my teeth**.

levantar-se	**1.** get up	tirar a roupa	**12.** get undressed
tomar banho (de chuveiro)	**2.** take a shower	tomar banho (de banheira)	**13.** take a bath
escovar os dentes	**3.** brush *my** teeth	ir para a cama/deitar-se	**14.** go to bed
limpar os dentes com fio dental	**4.** floss *my** teeth	dormir	**15.** sleep
fazer a barba	**5.** shave	preparar o café da manhã	**16.** make breakfast
vestir-se	**6.** get dressed	preparar o almoço	**17.** make lunch
lavar o rosto	**7.** wash *my** face	cozinhar/preparar o jantar	**18.** cook/make dinner
maquilar-se	**8.** put on makeup	tomar o café da manhã	**19.** eat/have breakfast
escovar o cabelo	**9.** brush *my** hair	almoçar	**20.** eat/have lunch
pentear o cabelo	**10.** comb *my** hair	jantar	**21.** eat/have dinner
fazer/arrumar a cama	**11.** make the bed		

*my, his, her, our, your, their

A. What does he do every day?
B. He _____s, he _____s, and he _____s.

A. What does she do every day?
B. She _____s, she _____s, and she _____s.

What do you do every day? Make a list.
Interview some friends and tell about their everyday activities.

ATIVIDADES COTIDIANAS II

A. Hi! What are you doing?
B. I'm **clean**ing **the apartment**.

limpar o apartamento/	**1.** clean the apartment/	
limpar a casa	clean the house	
varrer o chão	**2.** sweep the floor	
tirar o pó	**3.** dust	
passar o aspirador	**4.** vacuum	
lavar a louça	**5.** wash the dishes	
lavar a roupa	**6.** do the laundry	
passar a roupa	**7.** iron	
dar de comer ao bebê	**8.** feed the baby	
dar comida ao gato	**9.** feed the cat	
levar o cachorro para passear	**10.** walk the dog	

assistir televisão	**11.** watch TV
ouvir radio	**12.** listen to the radio
ouvir música	**13.** listen to music
ler	**14.** read
brincar	**15.** play
jogar basquete	**16.** play basketball
tocar violão	**17.** play the guitar
praticar piano	**18.** practice the piano
estudar	**19.** study
fazer ginástica	**20.** exercise

A. Hi, ...! This is ....
   What are you doing?
B. I'm _____ing. How about you?
A. I'm _____ing.

A. Are you going to _____ today?
B. Yes. I'm going to _____ in a
   little while.

What are you going to do tomorrow?
Make a list of *everything* you are
going to do.

A SALA DE AULA

A. Where's the **teacher**?
B. The **teacher** is *next to* the **board**.

A. Where's the **pen**?
B. The **pen** is *on* the **desk**.

professor/professora	**1.** teacher	quadro-negro/lousa	**18.** board
assistente do professor/	**2.** teacher's aide	giz	**19.** chalk
da professora		apoio de giz	**20.** chalk tray
aluno	**3.** student	apagador	**21.** eraser
cadeira	**4.** seat/chair	sistema de comunicação/	**22.** P.A. system/loudspeaker
caneta	**5.** pen	alto-falante	
lápis	**6.** pencil	quadro de avisos	**23.** bulletin board
borracha	**7.** eraser	percevejo	**24.** thumbtack
carteira	**8.** desk	mapa	**25.** map
mesa do professor /da professora	**9.** teacher's desk	apontador de lápis	**26.** pencil sharpener
livro	**10.** book/textbook	globo	**27.** globe
caderno/fichário	**11.** notebook	estante	**28.** bookshelf
folhas de papel	**12.** notebook paper	retroprojetor	**29.** overhead projector
papel quadriculado	**13.** graph paper	TV	**30.** TV
régua	**14.** ruler	tela (de projeção)	**31.** (movie) screen
calculadora	**15.** calculator	projetor de slides	**32.** slide projector
relógio	**16.** clock	computador	**33.** computer
bandeira	**17.** flag	projetor (de filmes)	**34.** (movie) projector

A. Is there a/an _____ in your classroom?*
B. Yes. There's a/an _____ next to/on the _____.

A. Is there a/an _____ in your classroom?*
B. No, there isn't.

Describe your classroom.
(There's a/an ....)

*With 12, 13, 19 use: Is there _____ in your classroom?

Levante-se.	**1.** Stand up.
Vá ao quadro-negro/à lousa.	**2.** Go to the *board*.
Escreva *seu nome*.	**3.** Write *your name*.
Apague *seu nome*.	**4.** Erase *your name*.
Sente-se.	**5.** Sit down./Take your seat.
Abra *o livro*.	**6.** Open *your book*.
Leia *a página oito*.	**7.** Read *page eight*.
Estude *a página oito*.	**8.** Study *page eight*.
Feche *o livro*.	**9.** Close *your book*.
Guarde *o livro*.	**10.** Put away *your book*.
Ouça *a pergunta*.	**11.** Listen to *the question*.
Levante *a mão*.	**12.** Raise *your hand*.
Responda.	**13.** Give *the answer*.
Trabalhem *em grupos*.	**14.** Work *in groups*.
Ajudem *uns aos outros*.	**15.** Help *each other*.

Faça *a lição de casa*.	**16.** Do *your homework*.
Traga *sua lição de casa*.	**17.** Bring in *your homework*.
Verifique *as respostas*.	**18.** Go over *the answers*.
Corrija *os erros*.	**19.** Correct *your mistakes*.
Entregue *a lição de casa*.	**20.** Hand in *your homework*.
Pegue *uma folha de papel*.	**21.** Take out *a piece of paper*.
Distribua *as provas*.	**22.** Pass out *the tests*.
Responda *às perguntas*.	**23.** Answer *the questions*.
Verifique *as respostas*.	**24.** Check *your answers*.
Recolha *as provas*.	**25.** Collect *the tests*.
Feche *as cortinas/as persianas*	**26.** Lower *the shades*.
Apague *as luzes*.	**27.** Turn off *the lights*.
Ligue *o projetor*.	**28.** Turn on *the projector*.
Assista *o filme*.	**29.** Watch *the movie*.
Tome notas.	**30.** Take notes.

You're the teacher! Give instructions to your students.

PAÍSES, NACIONALIDADES, E LÍNGUAS

A. Where are you from?
B. I'm from **Mexico**.

A. What's your nationality?
B. I'm **Mexican**.

A. What language do you speak?
B. I speak **Spanish**.

Country	Nationality	Language	Country	Nationality	Language
Afghanistan	Afghan	Afghan	Italy	Italian	Italian
Argentina	Argentine	Spanish	Japan	Japanese	Japanese
Australia	Australian	English	Jordan	Jordanian	Arabic
Bolivia	Bolivian	Spanish	Korea	Korean	Korean
Brazil	Brazilian	Portuguese	Laos	Laotian	Laotian
Cambodia	Cambodian	Cambodian	Latvia	Latvian	Latvian
Canada	Canadian	English/French	Lithuania	Lithuanian	Lithuanian
Chile	Chilean	Spanish	Malaysia	Malaysian	Malay
China	Chinese	Chinese	Mexico	Mexican	Spanish
Colombia	Colombian	Spanish	New Zealand	New Zealander	English
Costa Rica	Costa Rican	Spanish	Nicaragua	Nicaraguan	Spanish
Cuba	Cuban	Spanish	Panama	Panamanian	Spanish
(The) Dominican Republic	Dominican	Spanish	Peru	Peruvian	Spanish
Ecuador	Ecuadorian	Spanish	(The) Philippines	Filipino	Tagalog
Egypt	Egyptian	Arabic	Poland	Polish	Polish
El Salvador	Salvadorean	Spanish	Portugal	Portuguese	Portuguese
England	English	English	Puerto Rico	Puerto Rican	Spanish
Estonia	Estonian	Estonian	Romania	Romanian	Romanian
Ethiopia	Ethiopian	Amharic	Russia	Russian	Russian
France	French	French	Saudi Arabia	Saudi	Arabic
Germany	German	German	Spain	Spanish	Spanish
Greece	Greek	Greek	Taiwan	Taiwanese	Chinese
Guatemala	Guatemalan	Spanish	Thailand	Thai	Thai
Haiti	Haitian	Haitian Kreyol	Turkey	Turkish	Turkish
Honduras	Honduran	Spanish	Ukraine	Ukrainian	Ukrainian
Indonesia	Indonesian	Indonesian	(The) United States	American	English
Israel	Israeli	Hebrew	Venezuela	Venezuelan	Spanish
			Vietnam	Vietnamese	Vietnamese

A. What's your native language?
B. _____.
A. Oh. What country are you from?
B. _____.

A. Where are you and your husband/wife going on your vacation?
B. We're going to _____.
A. That's nice. Tell me, do you speak _____?
B. No, but my husband/wife does. He's/She's _____.

Tell about yourself:
  Where are you from?
  What's your nationality?
  What languages do you speak?
Now interview and tell about a friend.

A. Where do you live?
B. I live in an **apartment building**.

prédio de apartamentos	**1.** apartment (building)
casa térrea	**2.** (single-family) house
sobrado geminado	**3.** duplex/two-family house
casa geminada em fileira/vila	**4.** townhouse/townhome
condomínio	**5.** condominimum/condo
residência de estudantes	**6.** dormitory/dorm

trailer	**7.** mobile home/trailer
casa de fazenda	**8.** farmhouse
cabana	**9.** cabin
asilo de idosos	**10.** nursing home
abrigo	**11.** shelter
casa flutuante	**12.** houseboat

A. Town Taxi Company.
B. Hello. Please send a taxi to
   (address) .
A. Is that a house or an apartment?
B. It's a/an _____.
A. All right. We'll be there right
away.

A. This is the Emergency Operator.
B. Please send an ambulance to
   (address) .
A. Is that a private home?
B. It's a/an _____.
A. What's your name?
B. ....
A. And your telephone number?
B. ....

Tell about people you know and the
types of housing they live in.
Discuss:
   Who lives in dormitories?
   Who lives in nursing homes?
   Who lives in shelters?
   Why?

A. Where are you?
B. I'm in the living room.
A. What are you doing?
B. I'm *dusting** the **coffee table**.

*dusting/cleaning

mesa de centro	1. coffee table	televisão	15. television
tapete	2. rug	videocassete	16. video cassette recorder/VCR
chão	3. floor		
poltrona	4. armchair	aparelho de som	17. stereo system
mesa de canto	5. end table	alto falante/caixa acústica	18. speaker
abajur	6. lamp	namoradeira/	19. loveseat
cúpula	7. lampshade	sofá de dois lugares	
janela	8. window	planta	20. plant
cortina	9. drapes/curtains	quadro	21. painting
sofá	10. sofa/couch	moldura	22. frame
almofada	11. (throw) pillow	cornija	23. mantel
teto	12. ceiling	lareira	24. fireplace
parede	13. wall	grade/tela de lareira	25. fireplace screen
estante de TV e som	14. wall unit/entertainment unit	porta-retrato	26. picture/photograph
		estante de livros	27. bookcase

A. You have a lovely living room!
B. Oh, thank you.
A. Your _____ is/are beautiful!
B. Thank you for saying so.

A. Uh-oh! I just spilled coffee on your _____!
B. That's okay. Don't worry about it.

Tell about your living room.
(In my living room there's ....)

A. This **dining room table** is very nice.
B. Thank you. It was a gift from my *grandmother.**

**grandmother/grandfather/aunt/uncle/...*

mesa (de jantar)	**1.** (dining room) table		castiçal	**12.** candlestick
cadeira (de sala de jantar)	**2.** (dining room) chair		vela	**13.** candle
cristaleira	**3.** china cabinet		centro de mesa	**14.** centerpiece
porcelana/louça	**4.** china		saleiro	**15.** salt shaker
lustre	**5.** chandelier		pimenteiro	**16.** pepper shaker
buffet/tajer	**6.** buffet		manteigueira	**17.** butter dish
saladeira	**7.** salad bowl		carrinho de chá	**18.** serving cart
jarra (de água)	**8.** pitcher		bule de chá	**19.** teapot
sopeira	**9.** serving bowl		bule de café	**20.** coffee pot
bandeja	**10.** serving platter		leiteira	**21.** creamer
toalha de mesa	**11.** tablecloth		açucareiro	**22.** sugar bowl

---

[In a store]
A. May I help you?
B. Yes, please. Do you have
   _____s?*
A. Yes. _____s* are right over there.
B. Thank you.
With 4, use the singular.

[At home]
A. Look at this old _____
   I just bought!
B. Where did you buy it?
A. At a yard sale. How do you
   like it?
B. It's VERY unusual!

Tell about your dining room.
(In my dining room there's ....)

A SALA DE JANTAR : A MESA DE JANTAR

A. Excuse me. Where does the **salad plate** go?
B. It goes *to the left of* the **dinner plate**.

A. Excuse me. Where does the **soup spoon** go?
B. It goes *to the right of* the **teaspoon**.

A. Excuse me. Where does the **wine glass** go?
B. It goes *between* the **water glass** and the **cup and saucer**.

A. Excuse me. Where does the **cup** go?
B. It goes *on* the **saucer**.

prato de salada	**1.** salad plate	talheres	**silverware**
prato de pão	**2.** bread-and-butter plate	garfo de salada	**10.** salad fork
prato raso	**3.** dinner plate	garfo de entrada	**11.** dinner fork
prato fundo (de sopa)	**4.** soup bowl	faca	**12.** knife
copo de água	**5.** water glass	colher de chá	**13.** teaspoon
copo de vinho	**6.** wine glass	colher de sopa	**14.** soup spoon
xícara	**7.** cup	faca de manteiga	**15.** butter knife
pires	**8.** saucer		
guardanapo	**9.** napkin		

A. Waiter? Excuse me. This _____ is dirty.
B. I'm terribly sorry. I'll get you another _____ right away.

A. Oops! I dropped my _____!
B. That's okay! I'll get you another _____ from the kitchen.

Practice giving directions. Tell someone how to set a table.
(Put the ....)

A. Ooh! Look at that big bug!!
B. Where?
A. It's on the **bed**!
B. I'LL get it.

cama	**1.** bed
cabeceira	**2.** headboard
travesseiro	**3.** pillow
fronha	**4.** pillowcase
lençol com elástico	**5.** fitted sheet
lençol de cima	**6.** (flat) sheet
cobertor	**7.** blanket
cobertor elétrico	**8.** electric blanket
babado	**9.** dust ruffle
colcha	**10.** bedspread
acolchoado	**11.** comforter/quilt
pé (de cama)	**12.** footboard
persiana	**13.** blinds
mesa-de-cabeceira/ criado-mudo	**14.** night table/nightstand
despertador	**15.** alarm clock
rádio-relógio	**16.** clock radio
cômoda	**17.** chest (of drawers)
espelho	**18.** mirror
porta-jóias	**19.** jewelry box
toucador	**20.** dresser/bureau
cama de solteiro	**21.** twin bed
colchão	**22.** mattress
estrado (de molas)	**23.** box spring
cama de casal	**24.** double bed
cama tamanho queen-size	**25.** queen-size bed
cama tamanho king-size	**26.** king-size bed
cama beliche	**27.** bunk bed
bicama	**28.** trundle bed
sofá-cama	**29.** sofa bed/convertible sofa
divã	**30.** day bed
cama dobrável	**31.** cot
colchão de água	**32.** water bed
cama baldaquino/cama dossel	**33.** canopy bed
cama hospitalar	**34.** hospital bed

[In a store]

A. Excuse me. I'm looking for a/an _____.*
B. We have some very nice _____s. And they're all on sale this week.
A. Oh, good!

*With 13, use: Excuse me. I'm looking for _____.

[In a bedroom]

A. Oh, no! I just lost my contact lens!
B. Where?
A. I think it's on the _____.
B. I'll help you look.

Tell about your bedroom.
(In my bedroom there's ....)

A. I think we need a new **dishwasher**.
B. I think you're right.

lavadora de pratos	**1.** dishwasher	latas de mantimentos	**18.** canister
detergente de lavadora de pratos	**2.** dishwasher detergent	fogão	**19.** stove/range
detergente	**3.** dishwashing liquid	queimador/boca	**20.** burner
torneira	**4.** faucet	forno	**21.** oven
pia (de cozinha)	**5.** (kitchen) sink	pegador	**22.** potholder
triturador	**6.** (garbage) disposal	torradeira	**23.** toaster
esponja	**7.** sponge	porta-temperos	**24.** spice rack
palha de aço	**8.** scouring pad	abridor elétrico de latas	**25.** (electric) can opener
escova de lavar pratos	**9.** pot scrubber	livro de receitas	**26.** cookbook
escorredor de pratos	**10.** dish rack	geladeira	**27.** refrigerator
suporte de toalha de papel	**11.** paper towel holder	freezer	**28.** freezer
pano de prato	**12.** dish towel	geleira	**29.** ice maker
empacotadeira de lixo	**13.** trash compactor	forma de gelo	**30.** ice tray
armário	**14.** cabinet	ímã de geladeira	**31.** refrigerator magnet
microondas	**15.** microwave (oven)	mesa de cozinha	**32.** kitchen table
balcão/bancada	**16.** (kitchen) counter	jogo americano	**33.** placemat
tábua de carne	**17.** cutting board	cadeira de cozinha	**34.** kitchen chair
		cesto de lixo	**35.** garbage pail

[In a store]
A. Excuse me. Are your _____s still on sale?
B. Yes, they are. They're twenty percent off.

[In a kitchen]
A. When did you get this/these new _____(s)?
B. I got it/them last week.

Tell about your kitchen.
(In my kitchen there's ....)

ARTIGOS DE COZINHA

A. Could I possibly borrow your **wok**?
B. Sure. I'll get it for you right now.
A. Thanks.

wok	**1.** wok	batedeira (elétrica)	**23.** (electric) mixer
panela	**2.** pot	processador	**24.** food processor
panela/caçarola	**3.** saucepan	frigideira elétrica	**25.** electric frying pan
tampa	**4.** lid/cover/top	forma para waffles	**26.** waffle iron
frigideira	**5.** frying pan/skillet	grelha/chapa elétrica	**27.** (electric) griddle
assadeira com tampa	**6.** roasting pan	pipoqueira	**28.** popcorn maker
assadeira	**7.** roaster	liquidificador	**29.** blender
panela de banho-maria	**8.** double boiler	ralador	**30.** grater
panela de pressão	**9.** pressure cooker	batedor (de ovos) manual	**31.** (egg) beater
escorredor de macarrão	**10.** colander	concha	**32.** ladle
caçarola de pirex com tampa	**11.** casserole (dish)	concha de sorvete	**33.** ice cream scoop
forma de bolo	**12.** cake pan	forma de biscoito	**34.** cookie cutter
pirex	**13.** pie plate	peneira	**35.** strainer
tabuleiro	**14.** cookie sheet	espremedor de alho	**36.** garlic press
tigela	**15.** (mixing) bowl	abridor de garrafa	**37.** bottle opener
rolo de massa	**16.** rolling pin	abridor de latas	**38.** can opener
copo de medir	**17.** measuring cup	batedor	**39.** whisk
colher de medir	**18.** measuring spoon	descascador	**40.** (vegetable) peeler
cafeteira	**19.** coffeemaker	faca	**41.** knife
moedor de café	**20.** coffee grinder	espátula	**42.** spatula
chaleira	**21.** tea kettle	faca de descascar	**43.** paring knife
forninho	**22.** toaster oven		

A. What are you looking for?
B. I'm looking for the _____.*
A. Did you look in the drawers/ in the cabinets/next to the _____/............?
B. Yes. I looked everywhere!

*With 2, 4, 12–15, 41, use:
I'm looking for a _____.

[A Commercial]
Come to *Kitchen World*! We have everything you need for your kitchen, from _____s and _____s, to _____s and _____s. Are you looking for a new _____? Is it time to throw out your old _____? Come to *Kitchen World* today! We have everything you need!

What things do you have in your kitchen?
Which things do you use very often?
Which things do you rarely use?

A. Thank you for the **teddy bear.** It's a very nice gift.
B. You're welcome. Tell me, when are you due?
A. In a few more weeks.

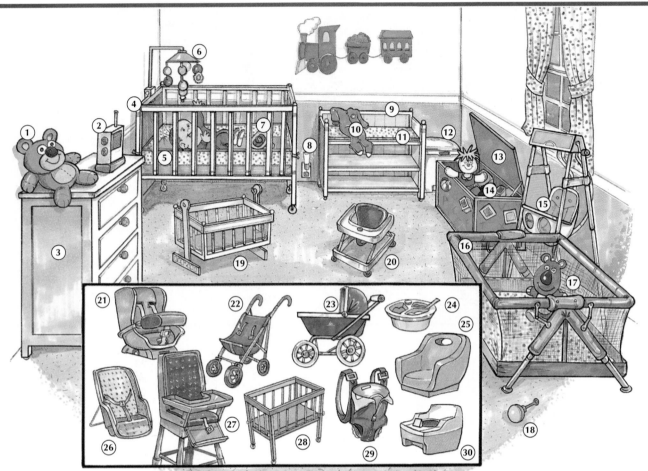

ursinho	**1.** teddy bear	cercado/chiqueirinho	**16.** playpen
babá eletrônica	**2.** intercom	bicho de pelúcia	**17.** stuffed animal
cômoda	**3.** chest (of drawers)	chocalho	**18.** rattle
berço	**4.** crib	berço	**19.** cradle
protetor	**5.** crib bumper	andador	**20.** walker
móbile	**6.** mobile	assento de carro	**21.** car seat
brinquedo de berço	**7.** crib toy	carrinho	**22.** stroller
luz noturna	**8.** night light	carrinho (coberto)	**23.** baby carriage
trocador	**9.** changing table/	prato térmico	**24.** food warmer
	dressing table	cadeirinha	**25.** booster seat
macacão	**10.** stretch suit	bebê-comforto	**26.** baby seat
colchonete do trocador	**11.** changing pad	cadeirão	**27.** high chair
cesta para fraldas usadas	**12.** diaper pail	berço portátil	**28.** portable crib
cesto/caixa de brinquedos	**13.** toy chest	canguru	**29.** baby carrier
boneca	**14.** doll	peniquinho	**30.** potty
balanço	**15.** swing		

A. That's a very nice _____.
   Where did you get it?
B. It was a gift from ....

A. Do you have everything you
   need before the baby comes?
B. Almost everything. We're still
   looking for a/an _____ and
   a/an _____.

Tell about your country:
   What things do people buy for a
   new baby?
   Does a new baby sleep in a separate
   room, as in the United States?

[1–12]
A. Do we need anything from the store?
B. Yes. Could you get some more **baby powder**?
A. Sure.

[13–17]
A. Do we need anything from the store?
B. Yes. Could you get another **pacifier**?
A. Sure.

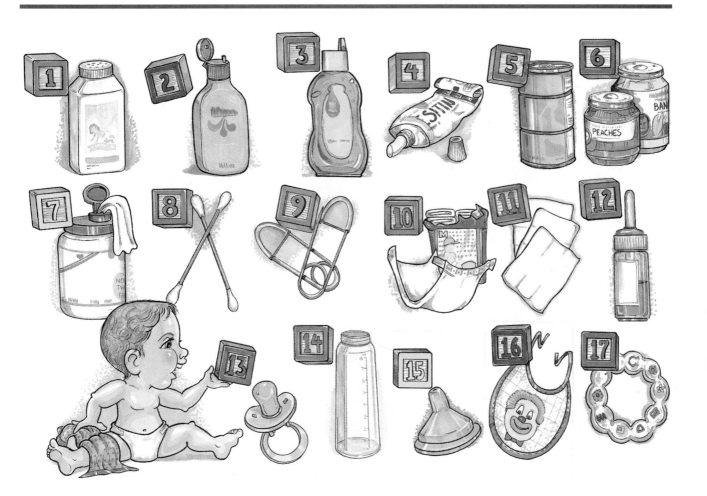

talco (de bebê)	**1.** baby powder	fraldas descartáveis	**10.** disposable diapers
loção (de bebê)	**2.** baby lotion	fraldas de tecido	**11.** cloth diapers
shampoo/xampu (de bebê)	**3.** baby shampoo	vitamina (gotas)	**12.** (liquid) vitamins
pomada	**4.** ointment	chupeta	**13.** pacifier
leite em pó	**5.** formula	mamadeira	**14.** bottle
comida/sopa de bebê	**6.** baby food	bico de mamadeira	**15.** nipple
lenços higiênicos	**7.** (baby) wipes	babador	**16.** bib
cotonetes	**8.** cotton swabs	mordedor	**17.** teething ring
alfinetes de fraldas	**9.** diaper pins		

[In a store]
A. Excuse me. I can't find the _____.*
B. I'm sorry. We're out of _____.* We'll have some more tomorrow.

[At home]
A. Honey? Where did you put the _____?
B. It's/They're in/on/next to the _____.

In your opinion, which are better: cloth diapers or disposable diapers? Why?
Tell about baby products in your country.

*With 13–17, use the plural.

A. Where's the **plunger**?
B. It's *next to* the **toilet**.

A. Where's the **toothbrush**?
B. It's *in* the **toothbrush holder**.

A. Where's the **washcloth**?
B. It's *on* the **towel rack**.

A. Where's the **mirror**?
B. It's *over* the **sink**.

desentupidor	**1.** plunger	torneira de água quente	**21.** hot water faucet
vaso sanitário	**2.** toilet	torneira de água fria	**22.** cold water faucet
caixa de descarga	**3.** toilet tank	copo/caneca	**23.** cup
assento sanitário	**4.** toilet seat	escova de dentes	**24.** toothbrush
purificador de ar	**5.** air freshener	suporte de escovas de dentes	**25.** toothbrush holder
suporte de papel higiênico	**6.** toilet paper holder	sabonete	**26.** soap
papel higiênico	**7.** toilet paper	saboneteira	**27.** soap dish
escova de vaso sanitário	**8.** toilet brush	porta-sabão (líquido)	**28.** soap dispenser
porta-toalha	**9.** towel rack	limpador de dentes	**29.** Water Pik
toalha de banho	**10.** bath towel	gabinete/armário	**30.** vanity
toalha de rosto	**11.** hand towel	cesto de lixo	**31.** wastebasket
toalha de lavar o rosto	**12.** washcloth/facecloth	box	**32.** shower
cesto de roupa	**13.** hamper	suporte de cortina de chuveiro	**33.** shower curtain rod
balança de banheiro	**14.** (bathroom) scale	chuveiro/ducha	**34.** shower head
prateleira	**15.** shelf	argolas de cortina	**35.** shower curtain rings
secador de cabelos	**16.** hair dryer	cortina de chuveiro	**36.** shower curtain
exaustor	**17.** fan	banheira	**37.** bathtub/tub
espelho	**18.** mirror	ralo	**38.** drain
armário de medicamentos	**19.** medicine cabinet/	tapete de banheira	**39.** rubber mat
	medicine chest	esponja	**40.** sponge
pia (de banheiro)	**20.** (bathroom) sink	tapete de banheira	**41.** bath mat/bath rug

A. [Knock. Knock.] Did I leave my glasses in there?
B. Yes. They're on/in/next to the _____.

A. *Bobby?*
B. Yes, Mom/Dad?
A. You didn't clean up the bathroom! There's toothpaste on the _____ and there's powder all over the _____!
B. Sorry, Mom/Dad. I'll clean it up right away.

Tell about your bathroom.
(In my bathroom there's ....)

[1–17]
A. Excuse me. Where can I find **toothbrush**es?
B. They're in the next aisle.
A. Thank you.

[18–38]
A. Excuse me. Where can I find **shampoo**?
B. It's in the next aisle.
A. Thank you.

escova de dentes	1. toothbrush
pente	2. comb
escova de cabelos	3. (hair) brush
barbeador	4. razor
gilete	5. razor blades
barbeador elétrico	6. electric razor/electric shaver
pedra pomes	7. styptic pencil
touca de banho	8. shower cap
lixa de unha	9. nail file
lixa de unha	10. emery board
cortador de unha	11. nail clipper
escova de unha	12. nail brush
tesoura	13. scissors
pinça	14. tweezers
grampinho/grampo de cabelo	15. bobby pins
clipe de cabelo	16. hair clips
prendedor de cabelo	17. barrettes
shampoo/xampu	18. shampoo
creme rinse/condicionador	19. conditioner/rinse

spray para cabelos/laquê	20. hairspray
pasta de dente	21. toothpaste
desinfetante bucal	22. mouthwash
fio dental	23. dental floss
creme de barbear	24. shaving creme
loção pós-barba	25. after shave lotion
desodorante	26. deodorant
talco	27. powder
loção para mãos	28. hand lotion
perfume/colônia	29. perfume/cologne
graxa para sapatos	30. shoe polish
esmalte de unhas	31. nail polish
acetona	32. nail polish remover

maquilagem makeup

base	33. base/foundation
blush/rouge	34. blush/rouge
baton	35. lipstick
sombra	36. eye shadow
delineador	37. eye liner
rímel	38. mascara

A. I'm going to the drug store to get a/an _____.*
B. While you're there, could you also get a/an _____?*
A. Sure.

*With 5, 13–38, use: get _____.

A. Do you have everything for the trip?
B. I think so.
A. Did you remember to pack your _____?
B. Oops! I forgot. Thanks for reminding me.

You're going on a trip. Make a list of personal care products you need to take with you.

MATERIAL DE LIMPEZA E LAVANDERIA

[1–17, 28–39]
A. Excuse me. Do you sell **broom**s?
B. Yes. They're at the back of the store.
A. Thanks.

[18–27]
A. Excuse me. Do you sell **laundry detergent**?
B. Yes. It's at the back of the store.
A. Thanks.

vassoura	**1.** broom	água sanitária	**20.** bleach
pá	**2.** dustpan	goma	**21.** starch
vassourinha	**3.** whisk broom	removedor de estática	**22.** static cling remover
espanador de penas	**4.** feather duster	limpador	**23.** cleanser
pano de pó	**5.** dust cloth	limpa-vidros	**24.** window cleaner
ferro de passar	**6.** iron	amoníaco	**25.** ammonia
tábua de passar	**7.** ironing board	lustra móveis	**26.** furniture polish
vassoura mágica	**8.** carpet sweeper	cera de assoalho	**27.** floor wax
aspirador de pó	**9.** vacuum (cleaner)	papel-toalha	**28.** paper towels
acessórios de aspirador de pó	**10.** vacuum cleaner attachments	cabide	**29.** hanger
saco de aspirador	**11.** vacuum cleaner bag	cesto para roupas	**30.** laundry basket
aspirador pequeno	**12.** hand vacuum	saco para roupas	**31.** laundry bag
esfregão de pó	**13.** (dust) mop/(dry) mop	tanque	**32.** utility sink
esfregão de esponja	**14.** (sponge) mop	escova pequena	**33.** scrub brush
esfregão	**15.** (wet) mop	esponja	**34.** sponge
máquina de lavar roupas/lavadora	**16.** washing machine/washer	balde	**35.** bucket/pail
secadora de roupas/secadora	**17.** dryer	lixo/lata de lixo	**36.** trash can/garbage can
sabão em pó	**18.** laundry detergent	cesto para lixo reciclável	**37.** recycling bin
amaciante de roupas	**19.** fabric softener	varal	**38.** clothesline
		prendedor de roupas	**39.** clothespins

A. How do you like this/these _____?
B. It's/They're great!

A. They're having a big sale at Dave's Discount Store this week.
B. Oh, really? What's on sale?
A. _[18–27]_ and _[1–17, 28–39]_ s.

Who does the cleaning and laundry in your home? What things does that person use?

A. When are you going to repair the **lamppost**?
B. I'm going to repair it next Saturday.

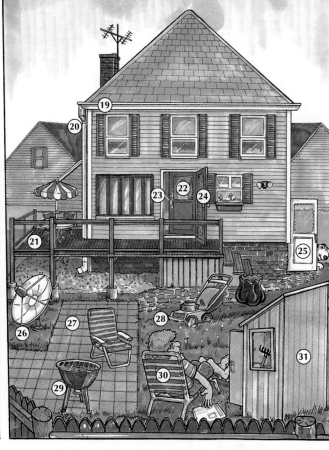

poste de luz	**1.** lamppost		porta da garagem	**17.** garage door
caixa de correio	**2.** mailbox		entrada de carro	**18.** driveway
entrada (da frente)	**3.** front walk		calha	**19.** gutter
degraus (da frente)	**4.** front steps		condutor da calha	**20.** drainpipe/downspout
varanda (da frente)	**5.** (front) porch		deck	**21.** deck
porta de inverno	**6.** storm door		porta dos fundos	**22.** back door
porta da frente	**7.** front door		fechadura	**23.** doorknob
campainha	**8.** doorbell		porta de tela	**24.** screen door
luz de entrada	**9.** (front) light		porta lateral	**25.** side door
janela	**10.** window		antena parabólica	**26.** satellite dish
tela de janela	**11.** (window) screen		pátio	**27.** patio
veneziana	**12.** shutter		cortador de grama	**28.** lawnmower
telhado	**13.** roof		churrasqueira	**29.** barbecue/(outdoor) grill
antena de TV	**14.** TV antenna		espreguiçadeira	**30.** lawn chair
chaminé	**15.** chimney		quartinho de ferramentas	**31.** tool shed
garagem	**16.** garage			

[On the telephone]
A. Harry's Home Repairs.
B. Hello. Do you fix _____s?
A. No, we don't.
B. Oh, okay. Thank you.

[At work on Monday morning]
A. What did you do this weekend?
B. Nothing much. I repaired my
_____ and my _____.

Do you like to repair things?
What things can you repair yourself?
What things can't you repair? Who repairs them?

O PRÉDIO DE APARTAMENTOS

A. Is there a **lobby**?
B. Yes, there is. Do you want to see the apartment?
A. Yes, I do.

saguão	**1.** lobby	ar condicionado	**11.** air conditioner
interfone	**2.** intercom	alarme de incêndio	**12.** fire alarm
porteiro eletrônico	**3.** buzzer	lixeira	**13.** garbage chute
caixa de correio	**4.** mailbox	lavanderia	**14.** laundry room
elevador	**5.** elevator	zelador	**15.** superintendent
porteiro	**6.** doorman	quarto de despejo	**16.** storage room
detector de fumaça	**7.** smoke detector	garagem	**17.** parking garage
olho mágico	**8.** peephole	estacionamento	**18.** parking lot
corrente de segurança (da porta)	**9.** (door) chain	terraço/varanda	**19.** balcony/terrace
		piscina	**20.** swimming pool
trava de segurança	**10.** dead-bolt lock	piscina com hidromassagem	**21.** whirlpool

---

[Renting an apartment]

A. Let me show you around the building.*
B. Okay.
A. This is the _____ and here's the _____.
B. I see.

*With 7–11, use:
  Let me show you around the apartment.

[On the telephone]

A. Mom and Dad? I found an apartment.
B. Good. Tell us about it.
A. It has a/an _____ and a/an _____.
B. That's nice. Does it have a/an _____?
A. Yes, it does.

Tell about the differences between living in a house and in an apartment building.

SERVIÇOS E CONSERTOS DOMÉSTICOS

A. Did you remember to pay the **carpenter**?
B. Yes. I wrote a check yesterday.

carpinteiro	**1.** carpenter	conta de gás	**12.** gas bill
reparador	**2.** handyman	conta de luz	**13.** electric bill
pintor	**3.** (house) painter	conta de telefone	**14.** telephone bill
limpador de chaminé	**4.** chimney sweep	conta de água	**15.** water bill
técnico de eletrodomésticos	**5.** appliance repair person	conta de óleo/aquecimento	**16.** oil bill/heating bill
técnico de TV	**6.** TV repair person	conta de TV a cabo	**17.** cable TV bill
chaveiro	**7.** locksmith	conta de controle sanitário	**18.** pest control bill
jardineiro	**8.** gardener	aluguel	**19.** rent
eletricista	**9.** electrician	taxa de estacionamento	**20.** parking fee
encanador	**10.** plumber	prestação de empréstimo de casa própria	**21.** mortgage payment
dedetizador	**11.** exterminator		

[1–11]
A. When is the _____ going to come?
B. This afternoon.

[12–21]
A. When is the _____ due?
B. It's due at the end of the month.

Tell about utilities, services, and repairs you pay for. How much do you pay?

A. Could I borrow your **hammer***?
B. Sure.
A. Thanks.

With 28–32, use: Could I borrow some _____s?

martelo	**1.** hammer	serra elétrica	**17.** power saw
chave de fenda	**2.** screwdriver	nível de bolha	**18.** level
chave estrela	**3.** Phillips screwdriver	plaina	**19.** plane
chave inglesa	**4.** wrench	caixa de ferramentas	**20.** toolbox
alicate	**5.** pliers	bandeja (de tinta)	**21.** (paint) pan
serra (para metal)	**6.** hacksaw	rolo (de pintura)	**22.** (paint) roller
machadinha	**7.** hatchet	brocha/pincel	**23.** paintbrush/brush
chave grifa	**8.** monkey wrench	tinta	**24.** paint
serrote	**9.** saw	tíner/solvente	**25.** paint thinner
furadeira manual	**10.** hand drill	lixa	**26.** sandpaper
arco de pua	**11.** brace	arame/fio	**27.** wire
talhadeira	**12.** chisel	prego	**28.** nail
espátula/raspadeira	**13.** scraper	parafuso	**29.** screw
morsa	**14.** vise	arruela	**30.** washer
furadeira elétrica	**15.** electric drill	parafuso	**31.** bolt
broca	**16.** (drill) bit	porca	**32.** nut

[1–4, 6–27]

A. Where's the _____?
B. It's on/next to/near/over/under the _____.

[5, 28–32]

A. Where are the _____(s)?
B. They're on/next to/near/over/under the _____.

Do you like to work with tools?
What tools do you have in your
home?

FERRAMENTAS DE JARDINAGEM E ARTIGOS DOMÉSTICOS

[1–16]
A. I can't find the **lawnmower**!
B. Look in the tool shed.
A. I did.
B. Oh! Wait a minute! I lent the **lawnmower** to the neighbors.

[17–32]
A. I can't find the **flashlight**!
B. Look in the utility cabinet.
A. I did.
B. Oh! Wait a minute! I lent the **flashlight** to the neighbors.

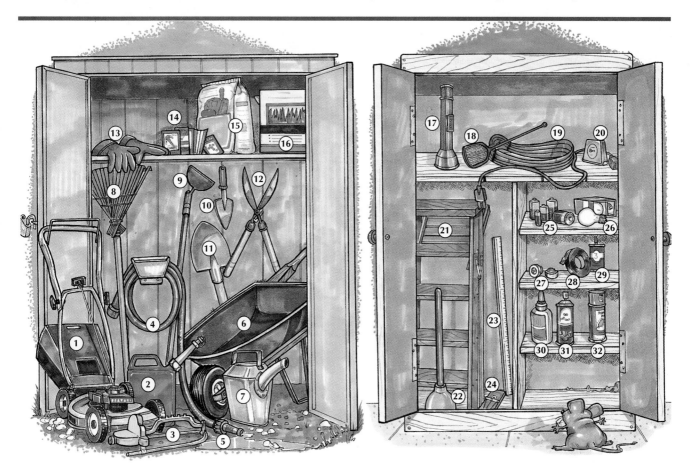

cortador de grama	**1.** lawnmower		lanterna	**17.** flashlight
galão de combustível	**2.** gas can		mata-mosca	**18.** fly swatter
aspersor	**3.** sprinkler		fio de extensão	**19.** extension cord
mangueira	**4.** (garden) hose		trena	**20.** tape measure
esguicho	**5.** nozzle		escada	**21.** step ladder
carrinho de mão	**6.** wheelbarrow		desentupidor	**22.** plunger
regador	**7.** watering can		régua (de jarda)	**23.** yardstick
ancinho	**8.** rake		ratoeira	**24.** mousetrap
enxada	**9.** hoe		pilhas	**25.** batteries
colher de jardineiro	**10.** trowel		lâmpadas	**26.** lightbulbs/bulbs
pá	**11.** shovel		fusíveis	**27.** fuses
tesoura (de jardim)	**12.** hedge clippers		fita isolante	**28.** electrical tape
luvas de jardinagem	**13.** work gloves		óleo (lubrificante)	**29.** oil
sementes de vegetais	**14.** vegetable seeds		cola	**30.** glue
fertilizante	**15.** fertilizer		inseticida	**31.** bug spray/insect spray
semente de grama	**16.** grass seed		inseticida (para baratas)	**32.** roach killer

[1–11, 17–24]
A. I'm going to the hardware store. Can you think of anything we need?
B. Yes. We need a/an _____.
A. Oh, that's right.

[12–16, 25–32]
A. I'm going to the hardware store. Can you think of anything we need?
B. Yes. We need _____.
A. Oh, that's right.

What gardening tools and home supplies do you have? Tell about how and when you use each one.

Números Cardinais / **Cardinal Numbers**

1	one	11	eleven	21	twenty-one	101	one hundred (and) one
2	two	12	twelve	22	twenty-two	102	one hundred (and) two
3	three	13	thirteen	30	thirty	1,000	one thousand
4	four	14	fourteen	40	forty	10,000	ten thousand
5	five	15	fifteen	50	fifty	100,000	one hundred thousand
6	six	16	sixteen	60	sixty	1,000,000	one million
7	seven	17	seventeen	70	seventy		
8	eight	18	eighteen	80	eighty		
9	nine	19	nineteen	90	ninety		
10	ten	20	twenty	100	one hundred		

A. How old are you?
B. I'm _____ years old.

A. How many people are there in your family?
B. _____.

Números Ordinais / **Ordinal Numbers**

1st	first	11th	eleventh	21st	twenty-first	101st	one hundred (and) first
2nd	second	12th	twelfth	22nd	twenty-second	102nd	one hundred (and) second
3rd	third	13th	thirteenth	30th	thirtieth	1000th	one thousandth
4th	fourth	14th	fourteenth	40th	fortieth	10,000th	ten thousandth
5th	fifth	15th	fifteenth	50th	fiftieth	100,000th	one hundred thousandth
6th	sixth	16th	sixteenth	60th	sixtieth	1,000,000th	one millionth
7th	seventh	17th	seventeenth	70th	seventieth		
8th	eighth	18th	eighteenth	80th	eightieth		
9th	ninth	19th	nineteenth	90th	ninetieth		
10th	tenth	20th	twentieth	100th	one hundredth		

A. What floor do you live on?
B. I live on the _____ floor.

A. Is this the first time you've seen this movie?
B. No. It's the _____ time.

MATEMÁTICA

Aritimética / **Arithmetic**

$$+\frac{2}{\frac{1}{3}} \qquad -\frac{8}{\frac{3}{5}} \qquad 4 \times 2 = 8 \qquad 10 \div 2 = 5$$

adição addition	subtração subtraction	multiplicação multiplication	divisão division
2 **plus** 1 **equals*** 3.	8 **minus** 3 **equals*** 5.	4 **times** 2 **equals*** 8.	10 **divided by** 2 **equals*** 5.

You can also say:* **is

A. How much is *two plus one*?
B. *Two plus one* equals/is *three*.

Make conversations for the arithmetic problems
above and others.

Frações / **Fractions**

 ¼ ⅓ ½ ⅔ ¾

one quarter/ one fourth	one third	one half/ half	two thirds	three quarters/ three fourths

A. Is this on sale?
B. Yes. It's _____ off the regular price.

A. Is the gas tank almost empty?
B. It's about _____ full.

Porcentagens / **Percents**

 25% 50% 75%  100%

twenty-five percent	fifty percent	seventy-five percent	one hundred percent

A. How did you do on the test?
B. I got _____ percent of the answers right.

A. What's the weather forecast?
B. There's a _____ percent chance of rain.

Research and discuss:
   What percentage of the people in your country live in cities?
   live on farms? work in factories? vote in national elections?

AS HORAS

 **2:00**

two o'clock

 2:15

two fifteen/
a quarter after *two*

 2:30

two thirty/
half past *two*

 **2:45**

two forty-five
a quarter to *three*

 **2:05**

two oh five

 **2:20**

two twenty/
twenty after *two*

 **2:40**

two forty/
twenty to *three*

 **2:55**

two fifty-five
five to *three*

A. What time is it?
B. It's _____.

A. What time does the movie begin?
B. At _____.

two a.m.

two p.m.

noon/
twelve noon

midnight/
twelve midnight

A. When does the train leave?
B. At _____.

A. What time will we arrive?
B. At _____.

Tell about your daily schedule:
    What do you do? When?
    (I get up at _____. I ....)
Do you usually have enough time to do things, or do you run
    out of time? Explain.
If there were 25 hours in a day, what would you do with the
    extra hour? Why?

Tell about the use of time in different cultures or countries
you are familiar with:
    Do people arrive on time for work? appointments? parties?
    Do trains and buses operate exactly on schedule?
    Do movies and sports events begin on time?
    Do workplaces use time clocks or timesheets to record
    employees' work hours?

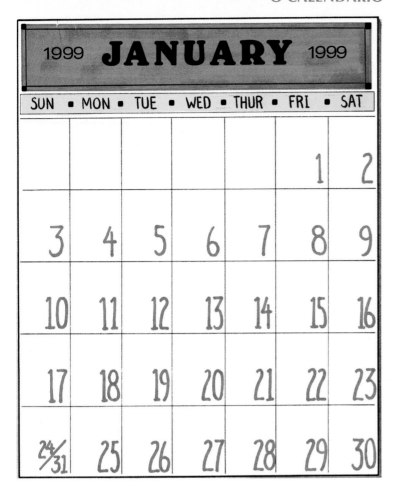

ano	1.	year
mil novecentos e noventa e nove		nineteen ninety-nine

mês	2.	month
janeiro		January
fevereiro		February
março		March
abril		April
maio		May
junho		June
julho		July
agosto		August
setembro		September
outubro		October
novembro		November
dezembro		December

dia	3.	day
domingo		Sunday
segunda-feira		Monday
terça-feira		Tuesday
quarta-feira		Wednesday
quinta-feira		Thursday
sexta-feira		Friday
sábado		Saturday

data	4.	date
2 de janeiro de 1999		January 2, 1999
2/01/99		1/2/99
dois de janeiro de (mil novecentos e) noventa e nove		January second, nineteen ninety-nine

A. What year is it?
B. It's _____.

A. What month is it?
B. It's _____.

A. What day is it?
B. It's _____.

A. What's today's date?
B. Today is _____.

When did you begin to study English?
What days of the week do you study English? (I study English on _____.)

When is your birthday? (My birthday is on _____.)
What are your favorite months of the year? Why?
What are your least favorite months of the year? Why?

A. Where are you going?
B. I'm going to the **appliance store**.

loja de eletro-domésticos	**1.** appliance store
agência de carros	**2.** auto dealer/car dealer
padaria/doceira	**3.** bakery
banco	**4.** bank
barbeiro	**5.** barber shop
livraria	**6.** book store
estação rodoviária	**7.** bus station
bar/lanchonete	**8.** cafeteria

berçário/creche	**9.** child-care center/day-care center
tintureiro/lavanderia	**10.** cleaners/dry cleaners
doceira/loja de donuts	**11.** donut shop
clínica/consultório	**12.** clinic
loja de roupas	**13.** clothing store
café	**14.** coffee shop
loja de informática	**15.** computer store

auditório/teatro	**16.** concert hall
loja de conveniência/venda	**17.** convenience store
copiadora	**18.** copy center
delicatessen/loja de queijos e frios	**19.** delicatessen/deli
loja de departamentos	**20.** department store
loja de descontos	**21.** discount store
drogaria/farmácia	**22.** drug store/pharmacy
floricultura	**23.** flower shop/florist
loja de móveis	**24.** furniture store
posto (de gasolina)	**25.** gas station/service station
mercearia	**26.** grocery store
cabeleireiro/salão de beleza	**27.** hair salon
loja de ferramentas	**28.** hardware store
academia de ginástica	**29.** health club/spa
hospital	**30.** hospital

A. Hi! How are you today?
B. Fine. Where are you going?
A. To the _____. How about you?
B. I'm going to the _____.

A. Oh, no! I can't find my wallet/purse!
B. Did you leave it at the _____?
A. Maybe I did.

Which of these places are in your neighborhood?
(In my neighborhood there's a/an …………)

A. Where's the **hotel**?
B. It's right over there.

 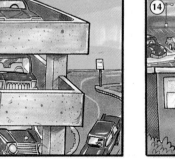  

hotel	**1.** hotel		museu	**9.** museum
sorveteria	**2.** ice cream shop		loja de discos	**10.** music store
joalheiro	**3.** jewelry store		boate/danceteria	**11.** night club
lavanderia automática	**4.** laundromat		parque	**12.** park
biblioteca	**5.** library		estacionamento coberto	**13.** (parking) garage
loja de maternidade	**6.** maternity shop		estacionamento aberto	**14.** parking lot
hotel para motoristas	**7.** motel		loja de animais	**15.** pet shop
cinema	**8.** movie theater			

loja de artigos de fotografia	**16.** photo shop	teatro	**24.** theater
pizzaria	**17.** pizza shop	loja de brinquedos	**25.** toy store
agência dos correios	**18.** post office	estação ferroviária	**26.** train station
restaurante	**19.** restaurant	agência de viagens	**27.** travel agency
escola	**20.** school	locadora de vídeos	**28.** video store
sapataria	**21.** shoe store	ótica	**29.** vision center/eyeglass store
shopping (center)	**22.** (shopping) mall	zoológico	**30.** zoo
supermercado	**23.** supermarket		

A. Is there a/an _____ nearby?
B. Yes. There's a/an _____ around the corner.

A. Excuse me. Where's the _____?
B. It's down the street, next to the _____.
A. Thank you.

Which of these places are in your neighborhood?
(In my neighborhood there's a/an ....)

A CIDADE

A. Where's the _____?
B. On/In/Next to/Between/Across from/
   In front of/Behind/Under/Over the _____.

lata de lixo	**1.** trash container		boca-de-lobo/bueiro	**11.** manhole
delegacia de polícia	**2.** police station		ponto de ônibus	**12.** bus stop
prisão/cadeia	**3.** jail		táxi	**13.** taxi/cab/taxicab
tribunal	**4.** courthouse		motorista de táxi	**14.** taxi driver/cab driver
banco	**5.** bench		ônibus	**15.** bus
poste de luz	**6.** street light		motorista de ônibus	**16.** bus driver
sorveteiro	**7.** ice cream truck		parquímetro	**17.** parking meter
calçada/passeio	**8.** sidewalk		inspetora de estacionamento	**18.** meter maid
meio-fio	**9.** curb		metrô	**19.** subway
rua	**10.** street		estação de metrô	**20.** subway station

poste	**21.**	utility pole	alarme de incêndio	**30.** fire alarm box
ponto de táxi	**22.**	taxi stand	cruzamento	**31.** intersection
cabine telefônica	**23.**	phone booth	policial	**32.** police officer
telefone público	**24.**	public telephone	travessia/faixa de pedestres	**33.** crosswalk
bueiro	**25.**	sewer	pedestre	**34.** pedestrian
placa (de nome) de rua	**26.**	street sign	semáforo/sinal de trânsito	**35.** traffic light/traffic signal
corpo de bombeiros	**27.**	fire station	caminhão de lixo	**36.** garbage truck
prédio de escritórios	**28.**	office building	banca de jornal	**37.** newsstand
guichê drive-thru	**29.**	drive-through window	vendedor ambulante/camelô	**38.** street vendor

[An Election Speech]
If I am elected mayor, I'll take care of all the problems we have in our city. We need to do something about our _____s. We also need to do something about our _____s. And look at our _____s! We REALLY need to do something about THEM! We need a new mayor who can solve these problems. If I am elected mayor, we'll be proud of our _____s, _____s, and _____s again! Vote for me!

Step outside. Look around. Describe everything you see.

Portuguese	Numbers	English
alto - baixo	**1–2**	tall – short
comprido - curto	**3–4**	long – short
grande - pequeno	**5–6**	large/big – small/little
alto - baixo	**7–8**	high – low
gordo - magro	**9–10**	heavy/fat – thin/skinny
pesado - leve	**11–12**	heavy – light
largo - apertado	**13–14**	loose – tight
rápido - lento	**15–16**	fast – slow
reto - torto	**17–18**	straight – crooked
liso - encaracolado	**19–20**	straight – curly
largo - estreito	**21–22**	wide – narrow
grosso - fino	**23–24**	thick – thin
escuro - claro	**25–26**	dark – light
novo - velho	**27–28**	new – old
jovem - velho	**29–30**	young – old
bom - mau	**31–32**	good – bad
quente - frio	**33–34**	hot – cold
macio - duro	**35–36**	soft – hard
fácil - difícil	**37–38**	easy – difficult/hard
liso - áspero	**39–40**	smooth – rough
arrumado - desarrumado	**41–42**	neat – messy
limpo - sujo	**43–44**	clean – dirty
barulhento - quieto	**45–46**	noisy/loud – quiet
casado - solteiro	**47–48**	married – single
rico - pobre	**49–50**	rich/wealthy – poor

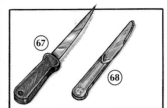

bonita/bela - feia	**51–52** pretty/beautiful – ugly	caro - barato	**61–62** expensive – cheap/inexpensive
bonito - feio	**53–54** handsome – ugly	elegante - simples	**63–64** fancy – plain
molhado - seco	**55–56** wet – dry	brilhante - opaco	**65–66** shiny – dull
aberto - fechado	**57–58** open – closed	afiado - cego (sem corte)	**67–68** sharp – dull
cheio - vazio	**59–60** full – empty		

[1–2]
A. Is your sister **tall**?
B. No. She's **short**.

1–2	Is your sister _____?		35–36	Is your pillow _____?
3–4	Is his hair _____?		37–38	Is today's homework _____?
5–6	Is their dog _____?		39–40	Is your skin _____?
7–8	Is the bridge _____?		41–42	Is your desk _____?
9–10	Is your friend _____?		43–44	Are the dishes _____?
11–12	Is the box _____?		45–46	Is your neighbor _____?
13–14	Are the pants _____?		47–48	Is your sister _____?
15–16	Is the train _____?		49–50	Is your uncle _____?
17–18	Is the path _____?		51–52	Is the witch _____?
19–20	Is his hair _____?		53–54	Is the pirate _____?
21–22	Is that street _____?		55–56	Are the clothes _____?
23–24	Is the line _____?		57–58	Is the door _____?
25–26	Is the room _____?		59–60	Is the pitcher _____?
27–28	Is your car _____?		61–62	Is that restaurant _____?
29–30	Is he _____?		63–64	Is the dress _____?
31–32	Are your neighbor's children _____?		65–66	Is your kitchen floor _____?
33–34	Is the water _____?		67–68	Is the knife _____?

A. Tell me about your ....
B. He's/She's/It's/They're _____.

A. Is your .... _____?
B. No, not at all. As a matter of fact, he's/she's/it's/they're _____.

Describe yourself.
Describe a person you know.
Describe one of your favorite places.

DESCREVENDO ESTADOS FÍSICOS E EMOÇÕES

A. You look **tired**.
B. I am. I'm VERY **tired**.

cansado	**1.** tired		doente	**9.** sick/ill
sonolento/com sono	**2.** sleepy		contente	**10.** happy
exausto	**3.** exhausted		eufórico/alegre	**11.** ecstatic
com calor/quente	**4.** hot		triste/descontente	**12.** sad/unhappy
com frio/frio	**5.** cold		infeliz/angustiado	**13.** miserable
esfomeado/com fome	**6.** hungry		satisfeito/contente	**14.** pleased
com sede/sedento	**7.** thirsty		desapontado/insatisfeito	**15.** disappointed
satisfeito/cheio	**8.** full		contrariado/aborrecido	**16.** upset

irritado	**17.** annoyed	preocupado	**25.** worried
frustrado	**18.** frustrated	com medo/apavorado	**26.** scared/afraid
zangado/com raiva	**19.** angry/mad	entediado	**27.** bored
furioso	**20.** furious	orgulhoso	**28.** proud
indignado/revoltado	**21.** disgusted	embaraçado	**29.** embarrassed
surpreso	**22.** surprised	envergonhado	**30.** ashamed
chocado	**23.** shocked	invejoso/com inveja	**31.** jealous
nervoso/inseguro	**24.** nervous	confuso	**32.** confused

A. Are you _____?
B. No. Why do you ask? Do I LOOK _____?
A. Yes. You do.

A. I'm _____.
B. Why?
A. ....

What makes you happy? sad? mad?
When do you feel nervous? annoyed?
Do you ever feel embarrassed? When?

FRUTAS

[1–22]

A. This **apple** is delicious!
   Where did you get it?
B. At *Shaw's Supermarket.*

[23–31]

A. These **grapes** are delicious!
   Where did you get them?
B. At *Farmer Fred's Fruit Stand.*

maçã	**1.** apple	côco	**12.** coconut	tangerina	**22.** tangerine
pêssego	**2.** peach	abacate	**13.** avocado	uvas	**23.** grapes
pêra	**3.** pear	melão cantalupo	**14.** cantaloupe	cerejas	**24.** cherries
banana	**4.** banana	melão	**15.** honeydew	ameixas secas	**25.** prunes
ameixa	**5.** plum		(melon)	tâmaras	**26.** dates
abricó	**6.** apricot	abacaxi	**16.** pineapple	(uvas) passas	**27.** raisins
nectarina	**7.** nectarine	melancia	**17.** watermelon	frutos do vacínio	**28.** blueberries
kiwi	**8.** kiwi	grapefruit/toranja	**18.** grapefruit	oxicocos	**29.** cranberries
mamão papaia	**9.** papaya	limão	**19.** lemon	framboesas	**30.** raspberries
manga	**10.** mango	lima	**20.** lime	morangos	**31.** strawberries
figo	**11.** fig	laranja	**21.** orange		

A. I'm hungry. Do we have any fruit?
B. Yes. We have _____s* and _____s.*

A. Do we have any more _____s?†
B. No. I'll get some more when I go to the supermarket.

What are your most favorite fruits?
What are your least favorite fruits?
Which of these fruits grow where you live?
Name and describe other fruits you are familiar with.

*With 14–18, use:
  We have _____ and _____.

†With 14–18, use:
  Do we have any more _____?

VEGETAIS E LEGUMES

A. What do we need from the supermarket?
B. We need **lettuce*** and **peas.**[†]

*1–12   [†]13–36

alface	**1.** lettuce	vagem	**14.** string bean/	batata	**25.** potato
repolho	**2.** cabbage		green bean	batata doce	**26.** sweet potato
aipo/salsão	**3.** celery	feijão-de-lima	**15.** lima bean	inhame/cará	**27.** yam
milho	**4.** corn	feijão preto	**16.** black bean	pimentão verde	**28.** green pepper
couve-flor	**5.** cauliflower	feijão roxo	**17.** kidney bean	pimentão vermelho	**29.** red pepper
brócoli	**6.** broccoli	couve-de-bruxelas	**18.** brussels sprout	beterraba	**30.** beet
espinafre	**7.** spinach	pepino	**19.** cucumber	cebola	**31.** onion
aspargo	**8.** asparagus	tomate	**20.** tomato	cebolinha (verde)	**32.** scallion/
berinjela	**9.** eggplant	cenoura	**21.** carrot		green onion
abobrinha	**10.** zucchini (squash)	rabanete	**22.** radish	cebola roxa	**33.** red onion
abobrinha redonda	**11.** acorn squash	cogumelo/	**23.** mushroom	cebola pequena	**34.** pearl onion
abobrinha marrom	**12.** butternut squash	champignon		nabo roxo	**35.** turnip
ervilha	**13.** pea	alcachofra	**24.** artichoke	nabo branco	**36.** parsnip

A. How do you like the
   [1–12] / [13–36] s?
B. It's/They're delicious.

A. *Johnny?* Finish your vegetables!
B. But you KNOW I hate
   [1–12] / [13–36] s!
A. I know. But it's/they're good
   for you!

Which vegetables do you like?
Which vegetables don't you like?
Which of these vegetables grow where
   you live?
Name and describe other vegetables
   you are familiar with.

A. I'm going to the supermarket to get **milk** and **soup**.*
   Do we need anything else?
B. Yes. We also need **cereal** and **soda**.*

*With 43, 44, 46, 49, and 55, use: a _____.

Laticínios	A. **Dairy Products**	Enlatados	B. **Canned Goods**	suco de abacaxi	27. pineapple juice
leite	1. milk	sopa	15. soup	suco de toranja	28. grapefruit juice
leite semi-desnatado	2. low-fat milk	atum	16. tuna fish	suco de tomate	29. tomato juice
leite desnatado	3. skim milk	legumes (enlatados)	17. (canned) vegetables	coquetel de frutas	30. fruit punch
leite achocolatado	4. chocolate milk	frutas (enlatadas)	18. (canned) fruit	suco de uva	31. grape juice
leitelho (desnatado)	5. buttermilk	Produtos Empacotados	C. **Packaged Goods**	suco de oxicoco	32. cranberry juice
suco de laranja	6. orange juice†	cereais	19. cereal	suco em caixa	33. juice paks
queijo	7. cheese	biscoitos/bolachas (doces)	20. cookies	refresco em pó	34. powdered drink
manteiga	8. butter	biscoitos/bolachas (salgadas)	21. crackers	Bebidas	E. **Beverages**
margarina	9. margarine	espaguete	22. spaghetti	refrigerantes	35. soda
creme azedo	10. sour cream	macarrão (oriental)	23. noodles	refrigerantes dietéticos	36. diet soda
queijo cremoso	11. cream cheese	macarrão	24. macaroni	água mineral	37. bottled water
queijo cottage	12. cottage cheese	arroz	25. rice		
iogurte	13. yogurt	Sucos	D. **Juice**		
ovos	14. eggs	suco de maçã	26. apple juice		

† Orange juice is not a dairy product, but is usually found in this section.

Aves	F. Poultry	costeleta	53. ribs	mariscos	67. clams
frango	38. chicken	Linguiças	54. sausages	caranguejos	68. crabs
coxas (e sobre-coxa)de frango	39. chicken legs	presunto	55. ham	lagosta	69. lobster
coxas de frango	40. drumsticks	bacon	56. bacon	**Padaria**	**I. Baked Goods**
peitos de frango	41. chicken breasts	**Peixes e Frutos do Mar**	**H. Seafood**	bolinhos	70. English muffins
asas de frango	42. chicken wings			bolo	71. cake
peru	43. turkey	PEIXES	FISH	pão sírio	72. pita bread
pato	44. duck	salmão	57. salmon	pãezinhos/bisnagas	73. rolls
		halibute (tipo de bacalhau)	58. halibut	pão (de forma)	74. bread
Carnes	**G. Meat**	linguado	59. flounder		
carne moída	45. ground beef	peixe-espada	60. swordfish	**Congelados**	**J. Frozen Foods**
rosbife	46. roast	hadoque	61. haddock	sorvete	75. ice cream
filé	47. steak	truta	62. trout	legumes congelados	76. frozen vegetables
carne para ensopados	48. stewing meat			refeições prontas congeladas	77. frozen dinners
pernil de cordeiro	49. leg of lamb	FRUTOS DO MAR	SHELLFISH		
bisteca de cordeiro	50. lamb chops	ostras	63. oysters	suco de limão congelado	78. frozen lemonade
carne de porco	51. pork	vieiras	64. scallops	suco de laranja congelado	79. frozen orange juice
bisteca de porco	52. pork chops	camarão	65. shrimp		
		mexilhões	66. mussels		

A. Excuse me. Where can I find __[1–79]__ ?

B. In the __[A–J]__ Section, next to the __[1–79]__ .

A. Thank you.

A. Pardon me. I'm looking for __[1–79]__ .

B. It's/They're in the __[A–J]__ Section, between the __[1–79]__ and the __[1–79]__ .

A. Thanks.

Which of these foods do you like?
Which foods are good for you?
What brands of these foods do you buy?

[1–70]

A. Look! _____ is/are on sale this week!

B. Let's get some!

Frios	**A. Deli**
rosbife	**1.** roast beef
mortadela	**2.** bologna
salame	**3.** salami
presunto	**4.** ham
peru	**5.** turkey
carne defumada	**6.** corned beef
queijo americano	**7.** American cheese
queijo suíço	**8.** Swiss cheese
provolone	**9.** provolone
mussarela	**10.** mozzarella
queijo cheddar (inglês)	**11.** cheddar cheese
salada de batata	**12.** potato salad
salada russa	**13.** cole slaw
salada de macarrão	**14.** macaroni salad
salada de frutos do mar	**15.** seafood salad

Salgadinhos	**B. Snack Foods**
batata chips	**16.** potato chips
salgadinhos de milho	**17.** corn chips
salgadinhos de tortilla	**18.** tortilla chips
salgadinhos de nachos	**19.** nacho chips
pretzels (rosca salgada)	**20.** pretzels
pipoca	**21.** popcorn
nozes variadas	**22.** nuts
amendoim	**23.** peanuts

Temperos	**C. Condiments**
ketchup/catchup	**24.** ketchup
mostarda	**25.** mustard
molhos temperados	**26.** relish
picles	**27.** pickles
azeitonas	**28.** olives
sal	**29.** salt

pimenta	**30.** pepper
temperos	**31.** spices
molho de soja	**32.** soy sauce
maionese	**33.** mayonnaise
óleo de cozinha	**34.** (cooking) oil
azeite/óleo de oliva	**35.** olive oil
vinagre	**36.** vinegar
molho de saladas	**37.** salad dressing

Chás e Café	**D. Coffee and Tea**
café	**38.** coffee
café descafeinado	**39.** decaffeinated coffee/ decaf coffee
chá preto	**40.** tea
chá de ervas	**41.** herbal tea
chocolate em pó/ achocolatados	**42.** cocoa/ hot chocolate mix

Farinhas e Açúcar	**E. Baking Products**
farinha	**43.** flour
açúcar	**44.** sugar
mistura para bolo	**45.** cake mix

Geléias	**F. Jams and Jellies**	filme de plástico	**62.** plastic wrap	cupons (de desconto)	**76.** coupons
geléia (firme)	**46.** jam	(de embalagem)		scanner	**77.** scanner
geléia cremosa	**47.** jelly	papel manteiga	**63.** waxed paper	balança	**78.** scale
geléia de laranja	**48.** marmalade	**Produtos Infantis**	**I. Baby Products**	caixa registradora	**79.** cash register
pasta de amendoim	**49.** peanut butter	cereais infantis	**64.** baby cereal	caixa	**80.** cashier
		leite em pó	**65.** formula	saco plástico	**81.** plastic bag
Produtos de Papel	**G. Paper Products**	sopa de bebê	**66.** baby food	saco de papel	**82.** paper bag
lenços de papel	**50.** tissues	lenços higiênicos	**67.** wipes	embalador	**83.** bagger/packer
guardanapos de papel	**51.** napkins	fraldas (descartáveis)	**68.** (disposable) diapers	(fila de) caixa expresso	**84.** express checkout (line)
papel higiênico	**52.** toilet paper			jornal popular	**85.** tabloid (newspaper)
copos descartáveis	**53.** paper cups	**Ração**	**J. Pet Food**		
pratos descartáveis	**54.** paper plates	ração de gato	**69.** cat food	revista	**86.** magazine
canudos	**55.** straws	ração de cão	**70.** dog food	chicletes	**87.** (chewing) gum
papel-toalha	**56.** paper towels			balas	**88.** candy
		Caixa	**K. Checkout Area**	cesto de supermercado	**89.** shopping basket
Artigos Domésticos	**H. Household Items**	corredor	**71.** aisle		
sacos de lanche	**57.** sandwich bags	carrinho de supermercado	**72.** shopping cart		
sacos de lixo	**58.** trash bags	comprador/cliente	**73.** shopper/customer		
sabonete	**59.** soap	balcão da caixa	**74.** checkout counter		
sabão em líquido	**60.** liquid soap	esteira	**75.** conveyor belt		
papel-alumínio	**61.** aluminum foil				

A. Do we need __[1–70]__ ?
B. No, but we need __[1–70]__ .

A. We forgot to get __[1–70]__ !
B. I'll get it/them.
 Where is it?/Where are they?
A. In the __[A–J]__ Section over there.

Make a complete shopping list of everything you need from the supermarket.
Describe the differences between U.S. supermarkets and food stores in your country.

A. Would you please get a **bag** of *flour* when you go to the supermarket?
B. A **bag** of *flour*? Sure. I'd be happy to.

A. Would you please get two **head**s of *lettuce* when you go to the supermarket?
B. Two **head**s of *lettuce*? Sure. I'd be happy to.

saco	**1.** bag	cacho/maço	**5.** bunch
barra	**2.** bar	lata	**6.** can
garrafa	**3.** bottle	caixa	**7.** carton
caixa	**4.** box	embalagem	**8.** container

dúzia	**9.** dozen*
espiga	**10.** ear
unidade	**11.** head
vidro	**12.** jar

* "a dozen eggs," NOT "a dozen of eggs."

forma/formas	**13.** loaf–loaves	cartucho/tablete	**18.** stick	1.9 litros	**22.** half-gallon
pacote	**14.** pack	pote	**19.** tub	3,8 litros	**23.** gallon
embalagem	**15.** package	473 ml	**20.** pint	litro	**24.** liter
rolo	**16.** roll	946 ml	**21.** quart	(453 g) libra	**25.** pound
pacote de seis unidades	**17.** six-pack				

[At home]
A. What did you get at the supermarket?
B. I got _____, _____, and _____.

[In a supermarket]
A. Is this checkout counter open?
B. Yes, but this is the express line. Do you have more than eight items?
B. No. I only have _____, _____, and _____.

Open your kitchen cabinets and refrigerator. Make a list of all the things you find.
What do you do with empty bottles, jars, and cans? Do you recycle them, reuse them, or throw them away?

colher de chá

colher de sopa

1 onça líquida -
1 oz lq. (29,57 ml)

1 xícara - oz 8 lq

teaspoon
tsp.

tablespoon
Tbsp.

1 (fluid) ounce
1 fl. oz.

cup
8 fl. ozs.

pint(473 ml)

946 ml

3.8 litros

pint
pt.
16 fl. ozs.

quart
qt.
32 fl. ozs.

gallon
gal.
128 fl. ozs.

A. How much water should I put in?
B. The recipe says to add one _____ of water.

A. This fruit punch is delicious! What's in it?
B. Two _____s of orange juice, three _____s
    of grape juice, and a _____ of apple juice.

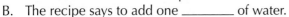

31 gramas

124 gramas

248 gramas

372 gramas

496 gramas

an ounce
oz.

a quarter
of a pound
¼ lb.
4 ozs.

half a pound
½ lb.
8 ozs.

three-quarters
of a pound
¾ lb.
12 ozs.

a pound
lb.
16 ozs.

A. How much roast beef would you like?
B. I'd like _____, please.

A. This chili tastes very good! What did you
    put in it?
B. _____ of ground beef, _____ of beans,
    _____ of tomatoes, and _____ of
    chili powder.

A. Can I help?
B. Yes. Please **cut up** the *vegetables.*

cortar	**1.** cut (up)	juntar ___ e ___	**14.** combine ___ and ___
picar	**2.** chop (up)	misturar ___ e ___	**15.** mix ___ and ___
fatiar	**3.** slice	cozinhar	**16.** cook
ralar	**4.** grate	assar	**17.** bake
descascar	**5.** peel	ferver	**18.** boil
misturar/mexer	**6.** stir/mix	grelhar	**19.** broil
bater	**7.** beat	fritar	**20.** fry
fritar mexendo	**8.** sauté	cozinhar no vapor	**21.** steam
derramar	**9.** pour	fritar mexendo (ovos)	**22.** scramble
cortar	**10.** carve	grelhar (churrasco)	**23.** barbecue/grill
encher ___ com ___	**11.** fill ___ with ___	fritar à chinesa	**24.** stir-fry
acrescentar ___ a ___	**12.** add ___ to ___	cozinhar no microondas	**25.** microwave
colocar ___ no ___	**13.** put ___ in ___		

[1–25] A. What are you doing?
　　　　B. I'm _____ing the …………

[16–25] A. How long should I _____ the …………?
　　　　 B. For ………… minutes/seconds.

What's your favorite recipe? Give instructions and use the
units of measure on page 52. For example:
　Mix a cup of flour and two tablespoons of sugar.
　Add half a pound of butter.
　Bake at 350° (degrees) for twenty minutes.

donut (rosquinha)	**1.** donut	Coca/Diet Coke/	**15.** Coke/Diet Coke/	sanduíche de	**27.** corned beef
bolinho	**2.** muffin	Pepsi/7-Up...	Pepsi/7-Up/...	carne defumada	sandwich
bagel (rosca)	**3.** bagel	suco de limão	**16.** lemonade	sanduíche de	**28.** BLT/bacon,
pão doce	**4.** bun	café	**17.** coffee	bacon, alface e	lettuce, and tomato
pastéis doces	**5.** danish/pastry	café descafeinado	**18.** decaf coffee	tomate	sandwich
biscoito/bolacha	**6.** biscuit	chá	**19.** tea	pão branco	**29.** white bread
croissant	**7.** croissant	chá gelado	**20.** iced tea	(de forma)	
hambúrguer	**8.** hamburger	leite	**21.** milk	pão de centeio	**30.** rye bread
cheesebúrguer	**9.** cheeseburger	sanduíche de atum	**22.** tuna fish sandwich	pão de trigo	**31.** whole wheat bread
cachorro quente	**10.** hot dog	sanduíche de	**23.** egg salad sandwich	integral	
taco (mexicano)	**11.** taco	salada de ovos		pão de centeio	**32.** pumpernickel
fatia de pizza	**12.** slice of pizza	sanduíche de	**24.** chicken salad	integral	
prato de chili	**13.** bowl of chili	salada de frango	sandwich	pão sírio	**33.** pita bread
(feijão com carne		misto	**25.** ham and cheese	um pãozinho	**34.** a roll
moída e pimenta)			sandwich	pão francês	**35.** a submarine roll
porção de	**14.** order of fried	sanduíche de	**26.** roast beef		
frango frito	chicken	rosbife	sandwich		

A. May I help you?
B. Yes. I'd like a/an [1–14] , please.
A. Anything to drink?
B. Yes. I'll have a small/medium-size/ large/extra-large [15–21] .

A. I'd like a [22–28] on [29–35] , please.
B. What do you want on it?
A. Lettuce/tomato/mayonnaise/mustard/...

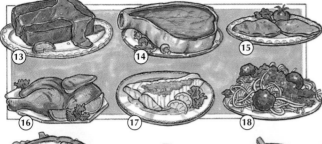

Entradas/Aperitivos	A. Appetizers		
coquetel de frutas	1. fruit cup/ fruit cocktail	asas de frango	4. chicken wings
suco de tomate	2. tomato juice	nachos (espécie de tortilla)	5. nachos
coquetel de camarão	3. shrimp cocktail	casca de batata assada	6. potato skins

Saladas	B. Salads		
salada mista	7. tossed salad/ garden salad	antepastos	10. antipasto
salada grega	8. Greek salad	salada Caesar	11. Caesar salad
salada de espinafre	9. spinach salad	bufê de saladas	12. salad bar

Prato Principal	C. Main Courses/Entrees		
torta de carne	13. meatloaf	frango assado	16. baked chicken
rosbife/contra filé	14. roast beef/ prime rib	peixe grelhado	17. broiled fish
filé de vitela	15. veal cutlet	espaguete com almôndegas	18. spaghetti and meatballs

Acompanhamentos	D. Side Dishes		
uma batata assada	19. a baked potato	arroz	22. rice
purê de batata	20. mashed potatoes	macarrão oriental	23. noodles
batatas fritas	21. french fries	legumes variados	24. mixed vegetables

Sobremesas	E. Dessert		
bolo de chocolate	25. chocolate cake	gelatina	28. jello
torta de maçã	26. apple pie	pudim/doce	29. pudding
sorvete	27. ice cream	sundae	30. ice cream sundae

[Ordering dinner]
A. May I take your order?
B. Yes, please. For the appetizer I'd like the _[1–6]_ .
A. And what kind of salad would you like?
B. I'll have the _[7–12]_ .
A. And for the main course?
B. I'd like the _[13–18]_ , please.
A. What side dish would you like with that?
B. Hmm. I think I'll have _[19–24]_ .

[Ordering dessert]
A. Would you care for some dessert?
B. Yes. I'll have _[25–29]_ /an _[30]_ .

Do you go to restaurants? Which ones? What do you order? Describe some popular desserts in your country.

CORES

A. What's your favorite color?
B. **Red.**

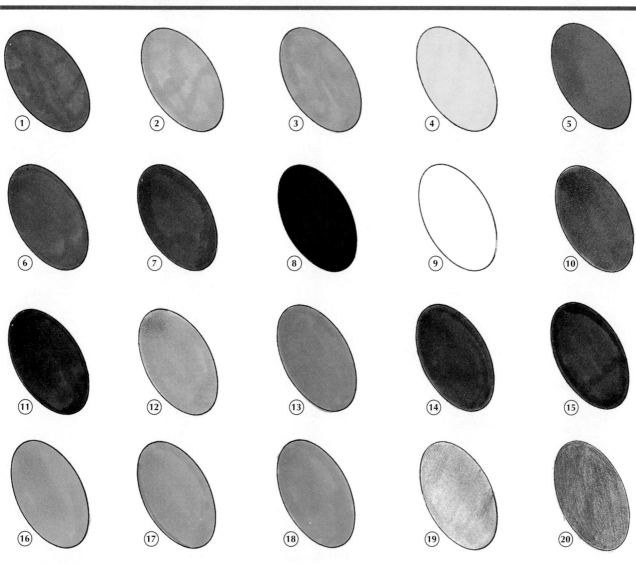

vermelho **1.** red	preto **8.** black	azul marinho **15.** navy blue
rosa **2.** pink	branco **9.** white	azul turquesa **16.** turquoise
laranja **3.** orange	cinza **10.** gray	rosa shock **17.** hot pink
amarelo **4.** yellow	marrom **11.** brown	verde neon **18.** neon green
verde **5.** green	bege **12.** beige	prateado **19.** silver
azul **6.** blue	verde claro **13.** light green	dourado **20.** gold
roxo **7.** purple	verde escuro **14.** dark green	

A. I like your _____ shirt.
   You look very good in _____.
B. Thank you. _____ is my favorite
   color.

A. My color TV is broken.
B. What's the matter with it?
A. People's faces are _____,
   the sky is _____, and the
   grass is _____!

Do you know the flags of different
   countries? What are the colors of
   the flags you know?
What color makes you happy? What
   color makes you sad? Why?

VESTUÁRIO

A. I think I'll wear my new **shirt** today.
B. Good idea!

camisa/camisa de manga comprida	**1.** shirt/long-sleeved shirt	jeans	**10.** (blue) jeans	paletó/blazer	**21** jacket/sports jacket/sports coat
camisa de manga curta	**2.** short-sleeved shirt	calça de veludo cotelê	**11.** corduroy pants/corduroys	jaqueta/blazer	**22.** jacket
camisa social	**3.** dress shirt	saia	**12.** skirt	jaquetão	**23.** blazer
camisa esporte	**4.** sport shirt	vestido	**13.** dress	terno	**24.** suit
camiseta pólo	**5.** polo shirt/jersey/sport shirt	macacão	**14.** jumpsuit	terno com colete	**25.** three-piece suit
		short/calças curtas	**15.** shorts	colete	**26.** vest
camisa de flanela	**6.** flannel shirt	malha/suéter	**16.** sweater	gravata	**27.** tie/necktie
blusa	**7.** blouse	malha de gola em V	**17.** V-neck sweater	gravata borboleta	**28.** bowtie
blusa de gola rolê	**8.** turtleneck	cardigã	**18.** cardigan sweater	smoking/traje a rigor	**29.** tuxedo
calças	**9.** pants/slacks	macacão	**19.** overalls	vestido (de baile/de gala)	**30.** (evening) gown
		uniforme	**20.** uniform		

pijama	**1.**	pajamas
camisola	**2.**	nightgown
camisão	**3.**	nightshirt
roupão/robe	**4.**	bathrobe/robe
chinelo	**5.**	slippers
camiseta/	**6.**	undershirt/
camiseta de baixo		tee shirt
cueca	**7.**	(jockey) shorts/
		underpants
cueca samba-	**8.**	boxer shorts
canção		
suporte atlético	**9.**	athletic supporter/
		jockstrap
ceroulas	**10.**	long underwear/
		long johns

calcinha	**11.**	(bikini) panties/
		underpants
calcinha	**12.**	briefs
soutien/sutiã	**13.**	bra
corpete	**14.**	camisole
combinação	**15.**	slip
anágua	**16.**	half slip
meia fina	**17.**	stockings
meia calça	**18.**	pantyhose
meia calça	**19.**	tights
meias	**20.**	socks
meia 3/4	**21.**	knee socks
sapatos	**22.**	shoes
sapatos de salto	**23.**	(high) heels
alto		

escarpim	**24.**	pumps
mocassin	**25.**	loafers
tênis	**26.**	sneakers
tênis	**27.**	tennis shoes
tênis	**28.**	running shoes
tênis cano alto	**29.**	high tops/
		high-top sneakers
sandálias	**30.**	sandals
chinelo de dedo	**31.**	thongs/flip-flops
(havaianas)		
botas	**32.**	boots
botina	**33.**	work boots
botas de caminhar	**34.**	hiking boots
botas de caubói	**35.**	cowboy boots
mocassins	**36.**	moccasins

[1–21]   A. I can't find my new _____.
         B. Did you look in the bureau/dresser/closet?
         A. Yes, I did.
         B. Then it's/they're probably in the wash.

[22–36]   A. Are those new _____?
         B. Yes, they are.
         A. They're very nice.
         B. Thanks.

camiseta	**1.** tee shirt	casaco	**12.** coat	galochas	**24.** rubbers
camiseta regata	**2.** tank top	capa/sobretudo	**13.** overcoat	luvas	**25.** gloves
blusão de moleton	**3.** sweatshirt	jaqueta	**14.** jacket	luvas (sem dedos)	**26.** mittens
calça de moleton	**4.** sweat pants	jaqueta	**15.** windbreaker	chapéu	**27.** hat
short	**5.** running shorts	jaqueta de esqui	**16.** ski jacket	boné	**28.** cap
short de tênis	**6.** tennis shorts	jaqueta de aviador	**17.** bomber jacket	boné	**29.** baseball cap
bermuda de lycra	**7.** lycra shorts	casaco tipo parka	**18.** parka	boina	**30.** beret
training	**8.** jogging suit/ running suit	jaqueta acolchoada	**19.** down jacket	chapéu de chuva	**31.** rain hat
		colete acolchoado	**20.** down vest	gorro	**32.** ski hat
collant	**9.** leotard	capa de chuva	**21.** raincoat	máscara de esqui	**33.** ski mask
collant de corpo	**10.** tights	poncho	**22.** poncho	protetor de orelha	**34.** ear muffs
testeira	**11.** sweatband	capa	**23.** trenchcoat	cachecol	**35.** scarf

[1–11]

A. Excuse me. I found this/these _____ in the dryer. Is it/Are they yours?

B. Yes. It's/They're mine. Thank you.

[12–35]

A. What's the weather like today?

B. It's cool/cold/raining/snowing.

A. I think I'll wear my _____.

JÓIAS, BIJUTERIAS E ACESSÓRIOS

A. Oh, no! I think I lost my **ring**!
B. I'll help you look for it.

A. Oh, no! I think I lost my **earrings**!
B. I'll help you look for them.

anel	**1.**	ring
anel (de noivado)	**2.**	engagement ring
aliança	**3.**	wedding ring/wedding band
brincos	**4.**	earrings
colar	**5.**	necklace
colar de pérolas	**6.**	pearl necklace/pearls
corrente	**7.**	chain
colar de contas	**8.**	beads
broche	**9.**	pin
relógio de pulso	**10.**	watch/wrist watch
bracelete/pulseira	**11.**	bracelet
abotoaduras	**12.**	cuff links
alfinete de gravatas	**13.**	tie pin/tie tack
prendedor de gravatas	**14.**	tie clip
cinto	**15.**	belt
chaveiro	**16.**	key ring/key chain
carteira	**17.**	wallet
porta-níquel	**18.**	change purse
bolsa	**19.**	pocketbook/purse/handbag
bolsa tiracolo	**20.**	shoulder bag
sacola	**21.**	tote bag
mochila escolar	**22.**	book bag
mochila	**23.**	backpack
pasta/maleta	**24.**	briefcase
guarda-chuva	**25.**	umbrella

[In a store]
A. Excuse me. Is this/Are these _____ on sale this week?
B. Yes. It's/They're half price.

[On the street]
A. Help! Police! Stop that man/woman!
B. What happened?!
A. He/She just stole my _____ and my _____!

Do you like to wear jewelry? What jewelry do you have?
In your country, what do men, women, and children use to carry their things?

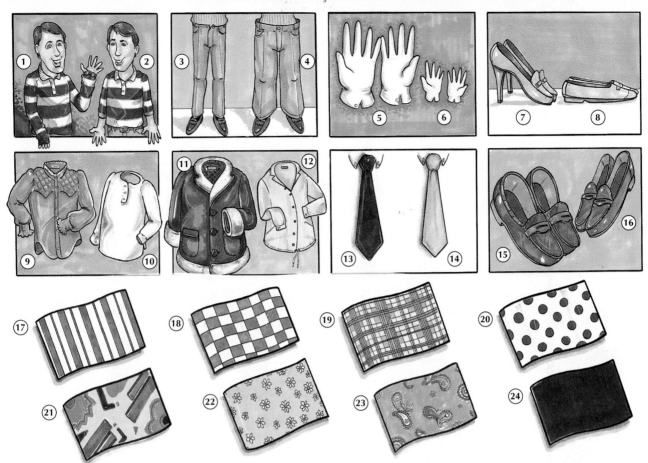

comprido - curto	**1–2**	long – short		listrado	**17.**	striped
apertado - folgado	**3–4**	tight – loose/baggy		quadriculado	**18.**	checked
grande - pequeno	**5–6**	large/big – small		xadrez	**19.**	plaid
alto - baixo	**7–8**	high – low		de bolas	**20.**	polka dot
elaborado - simples	**9–10**	fancy – plain		estampado	**21.**	print
pesado - leve	**11–12**	heavy – light		floral	**22.**	flowered
escuro - claro	**13–14**	dark – light		caximira	**23.**	paisley
largo - estreito	**15–16**	wide – narrow		azul liso	**24.**	solid *blue*

[1–2]
A. Are the sleeves too **long**?
B. No. They're too **short**.

1–2	Are the sleeves too _____?		9–10	Is the blouse too _____?
3–4	Are the pants too _____?		11–12	Is the coat too _____?
5–6	Are the gloves too _____?		13–14	Is the color too _____?
7–8	Are the heels too _____?		15–16	Are the shoes too _____?

[17–24]
A. How do you like this _____ tie/shirt/skirt?
B. Actually, I prefer that _____ one.

Describe your favorite clothing.

A. Excuse me. Where's the **store directory**?
B. It's over there, next to the **escalator**.

painel informativo	1. (store) directory	Setor de Utensílios	13. Housewares Department
escada rolante	2. escalator	Domésticos	
Setor de Roupa Masculina	3. Men's Clothing Department	Departamento de	14. Furniture Department/Home
balcão de perfumaria	4. Perfume Counter	Móveis e Decoração	Furnishings Department
balcão de joalheria	5. Jewelry Counter	Setor de Eletro-	15. Household Appliances
elevador	6. elevator	domésticos	Department
toalete masculino	7. men's room	Setor de Eletrônicos	16. Electronics Department
toalete feminino	8. ladies' room	Setor de Atendimento	17. Customer Assistance Counter/
bebedouro	9. water fountain	ao Cliente	Customer Service Counter
estacionamento	10. parking garage	lanchonete	18. snack bar
Setor de Roupas Femininas	11. Women's Clothing Department	Balcão de Pacotes	19. Gift Wrap Counter
Setor de Roupas Infantis	12. Children's Clothing Department	estacionamento	20. parking lot
		área de entregas	21. customer pickup area
		para clientes	

A. Pardon me. Is this the way to the
   _____?
B. Yes, it is./No, it isn't.

A. I'll meet you at/in/near/in front of
   the _____.
B. Okay. What time?
A. At *3:00*.

Describe a department store you
know. Tell what is on each floor.

A. May I help you?
B. Yes, please. I'm looking for a **TV**.

TV/aparelho de televisão	**1.** TV/television set		aparelho de som	**13.** stereo system/sound system
controle remoto	**2.** remote control (unit)		toca-fitas	**14.** tape recorder
videocassete	**3.** VCR/videocassette recorder		walkman	**15.** (personal) cassette player/ Walkman
fita de vídeo (virgem)	**4.** (blank) videotape		aparelho de som portátil	**16.** portable stereo system/boom box
vídeo (gravado)	**5.** video/(video)tape			
filmadora	**6.** camcorder/video camera		fita cassete	**17.** (audio) tape/(audio) cassette
toca-discos	**7.** turntable		CD	**18.** CD/compact disc
toca-fitas	**8.** tape deck		disco	**19.** record
aparelho de CD/CD player	**9.** CD player/compact disc player		fones de ouvido	**20.** set of headphones
amplificador	**10.** amplifier		rádio	**21.** radio
sintonizador	**11.** tuner		rádio de ondas curtas	**22.** shortwave radio
caixa (de som)	**12.** speaker		rádio-relógio	**23.** clock radio

A. How do you like my _____?
B. It's great/fantastic/awesome!

A. Which company makes a good _____?
B. In my opinion, the best _____ is made by ....

What video and audio equipment do you have or want?
In your opinion, which brands are the best?

COMPUTADORES, TELEFONES E MÁQUINAS FOTOGRÁFICAS

A. Can you recommend a good **computer**?*
B. Yes. This **computer** here is excellent.

*With 9, use: Can you recommend good _____?

computador	**1.** computer		aparelho de fax	**15.** fax machine
monitor	**2.** monitor		máquina fotográfica/câmera	**16.** camera
drive	**3.** disk drive		lente tele-objetiva/zoom	**17.** zoom lens
teclado	**4.** keyboard		maleta de aparelhos fotográficos	**18.** camera case
mouse	**5.** mouse		flash	**19.** flash attachment
impressora	**6.** printer		tripé	**20.** tripod
modem	**7.** modem		filme	**21.** film
disquete	**8.** (floppy) disk/diskette		projetor de slides	**22.** slide projector
software	**9.** (computer) software		tela portátil	**23.** (movie) screen
computador portátil	**10.** portable computer		máquina de escrever elétrica	**24.** electric typewriter
notebook	**11.** notebook computer		máquina de escrever eletrônica	**25.** electronic typewriter
telefone	**12.** telephone/phone		calculadora (de bolso)	**26.** calculator
telefone sem fio	**13.** portable phone/portable telephone		calculadora (de mesa)	**27.** adding machine
secretária eletrônica	**14.** answering machine		regulador de voltagem	**28.** voltage regulator
			transformador	**29.** adapter

A. Excuse me. Do you sell
_____s?†
B. Yes. We carry a complete line of
_____s.†

†With 9 and 21, use the singular.

A. Which _____ is the best?
B. This one here. It's made by
....

Do you have a camera? What kind
is it? What do you take pictures of?
Does anyone you know have an
answering machine? When you
call, what does the machine say?
How have computers changed the world?

A LOJA DE BRINQUEDOS

A. Excuse me. I'm looking for (a/an) _____(s) for my *grandson*.*
B. Look in the next aisle.
A. Thank you.

* *grandson/granddaughter/...*

jogo (de mesa)	**1.** (board) game	carrinho (miniatura)	**16.** matchbox car	prancha de skate	**31.** skateboard
blocos (de construção)	**2.** (building) blocks	caminhãozinho	**17.** toy truck	balanço	**32.** swing set
jogo de construção	**3.** construction set	autorama	**18.** racing car set	piscina de plástico/	**33.** plastic swimming
quebra-cabeça	**4.** (jigsaw) puzzle	trenzinho	**19.** train set	piscina infantil	pool/wading pool
bola	**5.** rubber ball	kit de modelismo	**20.** model kit	vídeogame	**34.** video game system
bola inflável	**6.** beach ball	kit de ciências	**21.** science kit	cartucho de vídeo-	**35.** (video) game
balde e pazinha	**7.** pail and shovel	giz de cera	**22.** crayons	game	cartridge
bambolê	**8.** hula hoop	canetão/pincel	**23.** (color) markers	videogame portátil	**36.** hand-held
corda de pular	**9.** jump rope	livro para colorir	**24.** coloring book		video game
boneca	**10.** doll	papel colorido	**25.** construction	walkie-talkie	**37.** walkie-talkie (set)
roupas de boneca	**11.** doll clothing	(de brincar)	paper	figurinhas	**38.** trading cards
casa de boneca	**12.** doll house	caixa de aquarelas	**26.** paint set	adesivos	**39.** stickers
móveis de casa de	**13.** doll house	massa de modelar	**27.** (modeling) clay	sabão para fazer	**40.** bubble soap
boneca	furniture	bicicleta	**28.** bicycle	bolhas	
boneco articulado	**14.** action figure	velocípede/triciclo	**29.** tricycle	casa de brinquedo	**41.** play house
bicho de pelúcia	**15.** stuffed animal	carrinho de puxar	**30.** wagon		

A. I don't know what to get my ....-year-old son/daughter for his/her birthday.
B. What about (a) _____?

A. Mom/Dad? Can we buy this/these _____?
B. No, *Johnny*. Not today.

What toys are most popular in your country?
What were your favorite toys when you were a child?

MONEY
DINHEIRO

Moedas / **Coins**

Name	Value	Written as:
1. penny	one cent	1¢ $ .01
2. nickel	five cents	5¢ $ .05
3. dime	ten cents	10¢ $ .10
4. quarter	twenty-five cents	25¢ $ .25
5. half dollar	fifty cents	50¢ $ .50
6. silver dollar	one dollar	$1.00

A. How much is a **penny** worth?
B. A penny is worth **one cent**.

A. *Soda* costs *seventy-five cents.*
   Do you have enough change?
B. Yes. I have a/two/three _____(s) and . . . .

Moedas / **Currency**

Name	We sometimes say:	Value	Written as:
7. (one-)dollar bill	a one	one dollar	$ 1.00
8. five-dollar bill	a five	five dollars	$ 5.00
9. ten-dollar bill	a ten	ten dollars	$ 10.00
10. twenty-dollar bill	a twenty	twenty dollars	$ 20.00
11. fifty-dollar bill	a fifty	fifty dollars	$ 50.00
12. (one-)hundred dollar bill	a hundred	one hundred dollars	$100.00

A. I need to go to the supermarket.
   Do you have any cash?
B. Let me see. I have a **twenty-dollar bill**.
A. **Twenty dollars** is enough. Thanks.

A. Can you change a **five-dollar bill/a five**?
B. Yes. I've got *five* **one-dollar bills**/*five ones*.

Written as	We say:
$1.20	one dollar and twenty cents
	a dollar twenty
$2.50	two dollars and fifty cents
	two fifty
$37.43	thirty-seven dollars and forty-three cents
	thirty-seven forty-three

How much do you pay for a loaf of bread? a hamburger?
   a cup of coffee? a gallon of gas?
Name and describe the coins and currency in your country.
   What are they worth in U.S. dollars?

talão de cheques	1. checkbook	cheque	10. check
registro de cheques	2. check register	ordem de pagamento	11. money order
extrato mensal	3. monthly statement	pedido de empréstimo	12. loan application
caderneta de conta bancária	4. bank book	caixa forte	13. (bank) vault
cheques de viagem	5. traveler's checks	cofre de aluguel	14. safe deposit box
cartão de crédito	6. credit card	caixa (funcionário)	15. teller
cartão magnético	7. ATM card	guarda de segurança	16. security guard
comprovante de depósito	8. deposit slip	caixa eletrônica	17. automatic teller (machine)/ ATM (machine)
comprovante de saque	9. withdrawal slip	funcionário do banco	18. bank officer

[1–7]
A. What are you looking for?
B. My _____. I can't find it/them anywhere!

[8–12]
A. What are you doing?
B. I'm filling out this _____.
A. For how much?
B. …………

[13–18]
A. How many _____s does the State Street Bank have?
B. …………

Do you have a bank account? What kind? Where?
Do you ever use traveler's checks? When?
Do you have a credit card? What kind? When do you use it?

O CORPO HUMANO

[1–23, 27–79]

A. My doctor checked my **head** and said everything is okay.

B. I'm glad to hear that.

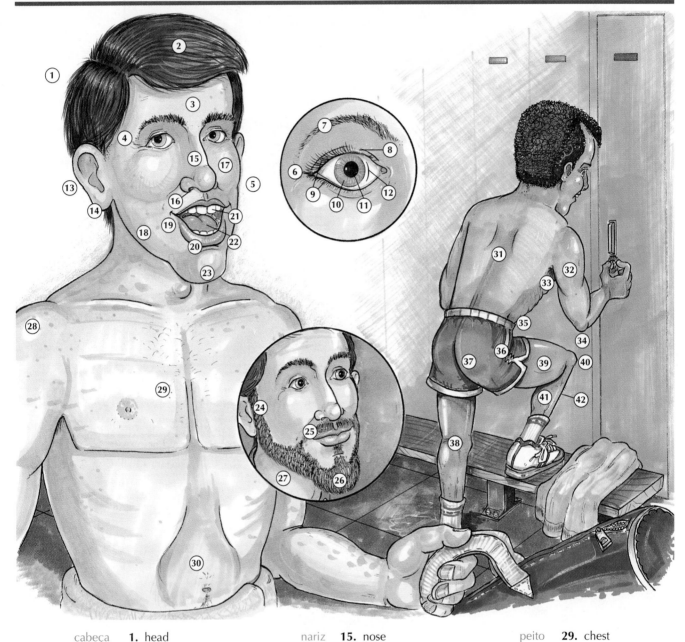

cabeça	**1.** head	nariz	**15.** nose	peito	**29.** chest
cabelo	**2.** hair	narina	**16.** nostril	abdome	**30.** abdomen
testa	**3.** forehead	bochecha	**17.** cheek	costas	**31.** back
têmpora	**4.** temple	maxilar	**18.** jaw	braço	**32.** arm
rosto	**5.** face	boca	**19.** mouth	axila	**33.** armpit
olho	**6.** eye	lábio	**20.** lip	cotovelo	**34.** elbow
sobrancelha	**7.** eyebrow	dente	**21.** tooth–teeth	cintura	**35.** waist
pálpebra	**8.** eyelid	língua	**22.** tongue	quadril	**36.** hip
cílios	**9.** eyelashes	queixo	**23.** chin	nádegas	**37.** buttocks
íris	**10.** iris	costeleta	**24.** sideburn	perna	**38.** leg
pupila	**11.** pupil	bigode	**25.** mustache	coxa	**39.** thigh
córnea	**12.** cornea	barba	**26.** beard	joelho	**40.** knee
orelha	**13.** ear	pescoço	**27.** neck	barriga da perna	**41.** calf
lóbulo (da orelha)	**14.** earlobe	ombro	**28.** shoulder	canela	**42.** shin

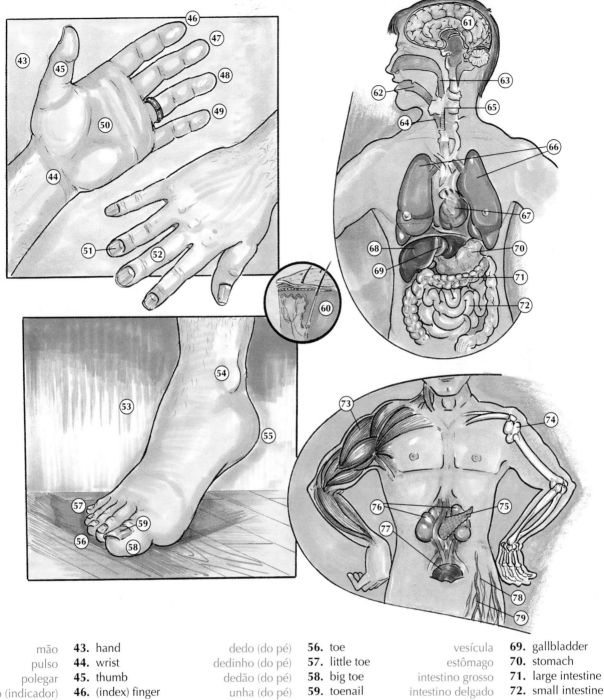

mão	**43.** hand	dedo (do pé)	**56.** toe	vesícula	**69.** gallbladder
pulso	**44.** wrist	dedinho (do pé)	**57.** little toe	estômago	**70.** stomach
polegar	**45.** thumb	dedão (do pé)	**58.** big toe	intestino grosso	**71.** large intestine
dedo (indicador)	**46.** (index) finger	unha (do pé)	**59.** toenail	intestino delgado	**72.** small intestine
dedo mediano	**47.** middle finger	pele	**60.** skin	músculos	**73.** muscles
dedo anelar	**48.** ring finger	cérebro	**61.** brain	ossos	**74.** bones
dedinho	**49.** pinky/little finger	garganta	**62.** throat	pâncreas	**75.** pancreas
palma	**50.** palm	esôfago	**63.** esophagus	rins	**76.** kidneys
unha (da mão)	**51.** fingernail	traquéia	**64.** windpipe	bexiga	**77.** bladder
nó (do dedo)	**52.** knuckle	coluna dorsal	**65.** spinal cord	veias	**78.** veins
pé	**53.** foot	pulmões	**66.** lungs	artérias	**79.** arteries
tornozelo	**54.** ankle	coração	**67.** heart		
calcanhar	**55.** heel	fígado	**68.** liver		

[1, 3–8, 13–23, 27–34, 36–60]
A. Ooh!
B. What's the matter?
A. { My _____ hurts!
     { My _____ s hurt!

[61–79]
A. My doctor wants me to have some tests.
B. Why?
A. She's concerned about my _____.

Describe yourself as completely as you can.
Which parts of the body are most important at school? at work? when you play your favorite sport?

DOENÇAS, SINTOMAS E FERIMENTOS

A. What's the matter?
B. I have a/an ___[1–19]___ .

A. What's the matter?
B. I have ___[20–26]___ .

dor de cabeça	**1.** headache	infecção	**10.** virus	verruga	**19.** wart
dor de ouvido	**2.** earache	viral/gripe		soluço	**20.** (the) hiccups
dor de dente	**3.** toothache	infecção	**11.** infection	calafrio/tremedeira	**21.** (the) chills
dor de estômago/	**4.** stomachache	urticária/erupção	**12.** rash	cólicas	**22.** cramps
dor de barriga		cutânea		diarréia	**23.** diarrhea
dor nas costas	**5.** backache	picada de inseto	**13.** insect bite	dor no peito	**24.** chest pain
dor de garganta	**6.** sore throat	queimadura de sol	**14.** sunburn	falta de ar	**25.** shortness of
febre	**7.** fever/	torcicolo	**15.** stiff neck		breath
	temperature	coriza	**16.** runny nose	laringite	**26.** laryngitis
resfriado	**8.** cold	sangramento nasal	**17.** bloody nose		
tosse	**9.** cough	cárie	**18.** cavity		

A. What's the matter?
B. { I feel __[27–30]__ .
    { I'm __[31–32]__ .
    { I'm __[33–38]__ ing.

A. What's the matter?
B. { I __[39–48]__ ed my ....
    { My .... is/are __[49–50]__ .

(sentir se) fraco	**27.** faint	chiar ao respirar	**35.** wheeze	esfolar	**43.** scrape
(estar com) tontura	**28.** dizzy	arrotar	**36.** burp	machucar	**44.** bruise
(estar com) náusea	**29.** nauseous	vomitar	**37.** vomit/throw up	queimar	**45.** burn
estufado	**30.** bloated	sangrar	**38.** bleed	quebrar	**46.** break–broke
congestionado	**31.** congested	torcer	**39.** twist	machucar	**47.** hurt–hurt
exausto	**32.** exhausted	contundir	**40.** sprain	cortar	**48.** cut–cut
tossir	**33.** cough	deslocar	**41.** dislocate	inchado	**49.** swollen
espirrar	**34.** sneeze	arranhar	**42.** scratch	(estar com) coceira	**50.** itchy

A. How do you feel?
B. Not so good./Not very well./Terrible!
A. What's the matter?
B. ...., ..., and ....
A. I'm sorry to hear that.

Tell about the last time you didn't feel well. What was
   the matter?
Tell about a time you hurt yourself. What happened?
   How?
What are the symptoms of a cold? a heart problem?

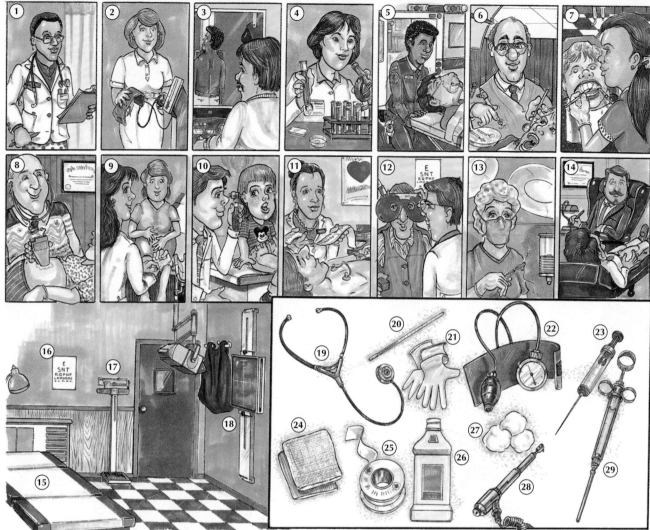

médico	**1.** doctor/physician	cardiologista	**11.** cardiologist	aparelho de medir	**22.** blood pressure
enfermeira(o)	**2.** nurse	optometrista	**12.** optometrist	pressão	gauge
técnico de raio-X	**3.** X-ray technician	cirurgião/cirurgiã	**13.** surgeon	agulha/seringa	**23.** needle/syringe
técnico de laboratório	**4.** lab technician	psiquiatra	**14.** psychiatrist	bandagens/gaze	**24.** bandages/gauze
atendente de	**5.** EMT/emergency	mesa de exame	**15.** examination table	fita adesiva	**25.** adhesive tape
emergência médica	medical technician	quadro de exame	**16.** eye chart	álcool	**26.** alcohol
dentista	**6.** dentist	de vista		bolas de algodão	**27.** cotton balls
técnico de odontologia	**7.** (oral) hygienist	balança	**17.** scale	broca de dentista	**28.** drill
obstetra	**8.** obstetrician	aparelho de raio-X	**18.** X-ray machine	anestesia/	**29.** anesthetic/
ginecologista	**9.** gynecologist	estetoscópio	**19.** stethoscope	anestésico	Novocaine
pediatra	**10.** pediatrician	termômetro	**20.** thermometer		
		luvas	**21.** gloves		

[1–14]
A. What do you do?
B. I'm a/an _____.

[15–18]
A. Please step over here to the _____.
B. Okay.

[19–29]
A. Please hand me the _____.
B. Here you are.

Where do you go for medical care? How often? Who examines you? What does he/she do?

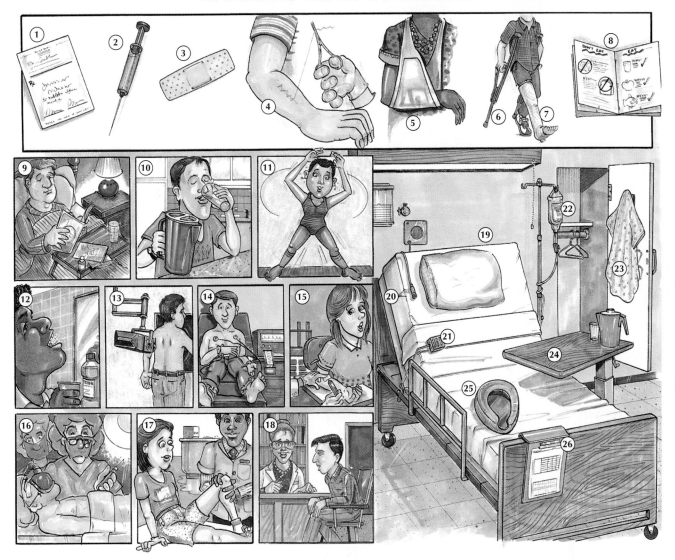

receita	**1.** prescription	beber bastante líquido	**10.** drink fluids	(psico)-terapia	**18.** counseling
injeção	**2.** injection/shot	fazer ginástica	**11.** exercise	cama hospitalar	**19.** hospital bed
bandaid	**3.** bandaid	gargarejar	**12.** gargle	botão de chamada	**20.** call button
pontos	**4.** stitches	raios-X	**13** X-rays	comando da cama	**21.** bed control
tipóia	**5.** sling	exames	**14.** tests	soro	**22.** I.V.
muleta	**6.** crutches	exames de sangue	**15.** blood work/	avental hospitalar	**23.** hospital gown
gesso	**7.** cast		blood tests	mesa de cama	**24.** bed table
dieta	**8.** diet	cirurgia	**16.** surgery	comadre	**25.** bed pan
descansar na cama	**9.** rest in bed	fisioterapia	**17.** physical therapy	prontuário	**26.** medical chart

[1–8]
A. What did the doctor do?
B. She/He gave me (a/an) _____.

[9–18]
A. What did the doctor say?
B. { She/He told me to [9–12].
    { She/He told me I need [13–18].

[19–26]
A. This is your _____.
B. I see.

When did you have your last medical checkup?
What did the doctor say?

Have you ever been in the hospital?
When? Why? Tell about your experience.

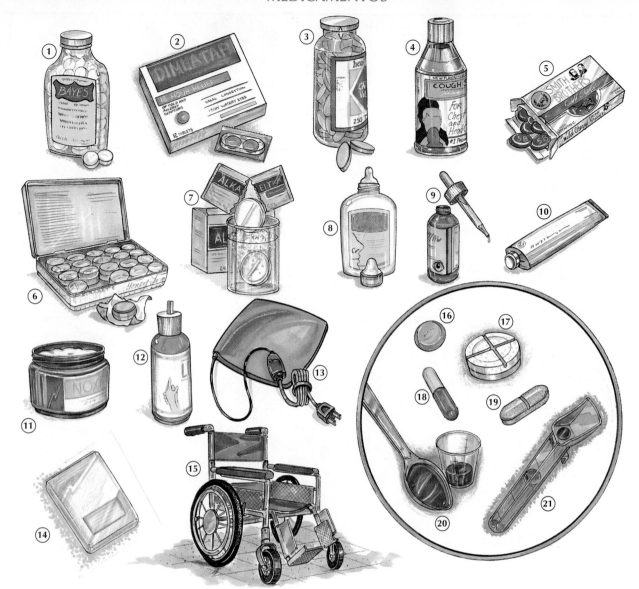

aspirina	1. aspirin	descongestionante	8. decongestant	cadeira de rodas	15. wheelchair
remédios para a gripe	2. cold tablets	nasal/spray nasal	spray/nasal spray	comprimido/pílula	16. pill
vitaminas	3. vitamins	colírio	9. eye drops	comprimido/pílula	17. tablet
xarope para tosse	4. cough syrup	pomada	10. ointment	cápsula	18. capsule
pastilhas para tosse	5. cough drops	creme	11. creme	cápsula	19. caplet
pastilhas de garganta	6. throat lozenges	loção	12. lotion	medida de colher de chá	20. teaspoon
remédio efervescente	7. antacid tablets	bolsa quente	13. heating pad	medida de colher de sopa	21. tablespoon
anti-ácido		bolsa de gelo	14. ice pack		

[1–15]   A. What did the doctor say?
          B. { She/He told me to take [1–4] .
               She/He told me to use (a/an) [5–15] .

[16–21]   A. What's the dosage?
          B. One _____, every three hours.

What medicines do you take or use?   Describe any medical treatments or medicines in your
For what ailments?   country that are different from the ones in these lessons.

carta	**1.** letter	selo	**11.** stamp	selo	**22.** stamp/postage
cartão postal	**2.** postcard	folha de selos	**12.** sheet of stamps	carimbo postal	**23.** postmark
aerograma	**3.** air letter/ aerogramme	rolo de selos	**13.** roll of stamps	escaninho	**24.** mail slot
encomenda	**4.** package/parcel	cartela de selos	**14.** book of stamps	guichê	**25.** window
carta normal	**5.** first class	vale postal	**15.** money order	funcionário dos	**26.** postal worker/
carta via aérea	**6.** air mail	formulário de	**16.** change-of-address	correios	postal clerk
encomenda	**7.** parcel post	mudança de endereço	form	balança	**27.** scale
material impresso	**8.** book rate/third class	formulário de registro de serviços especiais	**17.** selective service registration form	máquina de selos	**28.** stamp machine
				carro do correio	**29.** mail truck
carta registrada	**9.** registered mail	envelope	**18.** envelope	caixa de correio	**30.** mailbox
entrega expressa (sedex)	**10.** express mail/ overnight mail	endereço	**19.** address	carteiro	**31.** letter carrier/ mail carrier
		código postal (CEP)	**20.** zip code	malote	**32.** mail bag
		endereço de remetente	**21.** return address		

[1–4]
A. Where are you going?
B. To the post office.
I have to mail a/an _____.

[5–10]
A. How do you want to send it?
B. _____, please.

[11–17]
A. Next!
B. I'd like a _____, please.
A. Here you are.

[19–22]
A. Do you want me to mail this letter for you?
B. Yes, thanks.
A. Oops! You forgot the _____!

What time does your letter carrier deliver your mail? Does he/she drive a mail truck or carry a mail bag and walk?

Describe the post office you use:
How many postal windows are there?
Is there a stamp machine?
Are the postal workers friendly?

Tell about the postal system in your country.

bibliotecário	**1.** librarian		setor da mídia	**16.** media section
balcão de saída	**2.** checkout desk		fita de vídeo	**17.** videotape
assistente de biblioteca	**3.** library assistant		disco	**18.** record
microfilme	**4.** microfilm		fita cassete	**19.** tape
microficha	**5.** microfiche		disquete	**20.** computer diskette
catálogo de fichas	**6.** card catalog		seção de periódicos	**21.** periodicals section
catálogo online	**7.** online catalog		jornal	**22.** newspaper
estantes	**8.** shelves		revista	**23.** magazine
balcão de informações	**9.** information desk		periódico	**24.** journal
copiadora/máquina de xerox	**10.** copier/(photo)copy machine		ficha de catálogo	**25.** call card
bibliotecária de consultas	**11.** reference librarian		código de referência	**26.** call number
setor de consultas	**12.** reference section		autor	**27.** author
atlas	**13.** atlas		título	**28.** title
enciclopédia	**14.** encyclopedia		assunto	**29.** subject
dicionário	**15.** dictionary		cartão de biblioteca	**30.** library card

[1–11]

A. Excuse me. Where's/
Where are the _____?

B. Over there, at/near/next to
the _____.

[12–24]

A. Excuse me. Where can I find
a/an [13–15, 17–20, 22–24] ?

B. Look in the [12, 16, 21] over
there.

[27–29]

A. May I help you?

B. Yes, please. I'm having
trouble finding a book.

A. Do you know the _____?

B. Yes. …………

Do you go to a library? Which one? What does this library have? Describe how you use the library.

secreta
enferma
sala do orientad
cantina/b
direto
sala de au
armário pessc
laboratório de língu
laboratório
ciênci

nge   orientador   **20.** guidance counselor
ium   monitor(a) de cantina   **21.** lunchroom monitor
            funcionário(a) de   **22.** cafeteria worker
            cantina
            instrutor de   **23** driver's ed instructor
            auto-escola
            professor/professora   **24.** teacher
            treinador   **25.** coach
principal   zelador   **26.** custodian
urse

[1–16] A. Where
        B. I'm going to the _____.*
        A. Do you have a hall pass?
        B. Yes. Here it is.
        With 6 and 7, use: I'm going to my _____.

[17–26] A. Who's that?
        B. That's the new

Describe the school where you study English.
Tell about the rooms, offices, and people.

Tell about differences between schools in the United States
and in your country.

MATÉRIAS ESCOLARES E ATIVIDADES EXTRA-CURRICULARES

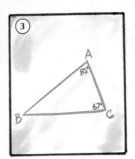

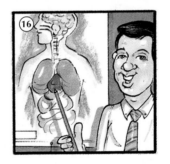

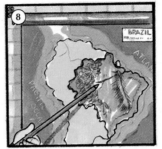

matemática	**1.** math/mathematics	ciências	**9.** science	oficina técnica	**17.** industrial arts/shop
álgebra	**2.** algebra	biologia	**10.** biology	curso de auto-escola	**18.** driver's education/ driver's ed
geometria	**3.** geometry	química	**11.** chemistry		
trigonometria	**4.** trigonometry	física	**12.** physics	datilografia	**19.** typing
cálculo	**5.** calculus	espanhol	**13.** Spanish	artes	**20.** art
inglês	**6.** English	francês	**14.** French	música	**21.** music
história	**7.** history	artes domésticas	**15.** home economics		
geografia	**8.** geography	saúde e higiene	**16.** health		

banda	**22.** band	jornal da escola	**27.** school newspaper
orquestra	**23.** orchestra	anuário da escola	**28.** yearbook
coral	**24.** choir/chorus	revista literária	**29.** literary magazine
teatro	**25.** drama	comissão de alunos	**30.** student government
futebol (americano)	**26.** football		

[1–21]

A. What do you have next period?

B. _____. How about you?

A. _____.

B. There's the bell. I've got to go.

[22–30]

A. Are you going home right after school?

B. { No. I have __[22–26]__ practice.
{ No. I have a __[27–30]__ meeting.

What is/was your favorite subject? Why? What extracurricular activities do/did you participate in?

PROFISSÕES I

A. What do you do?
B. I'm an **accountant**. How about you?
A. I'm a **carpenter**.

contador	**1.** accountant	montador	**6.** assembler	motorista de ônibus	**11.** bus driver
ator	**2.** actor	padeiro	**7.** baker	açougueiro	**12.** butcher
atriz	**3.** actress	barbeiro	**8.** barber	carpinteiro	**13.** carpenter
arquiteto	**4.** architect	guarda-livros	**9.** bookkeeper	caixa	**14.** cashier
artista plástico	**5.** artist	pedreiro	**10.** bricklayer/mason	cozinheiro	**15.** chef/cook

programador	16. computer programmer	entregador	21. delivery person	jardineiro	27. gardener
operário de construção civil	17. construction worker	eletricista	22. electrician	cabeleireiro	28. hairdresser
		agricultor	23. farmer	empregada doméstica	29. housekeeper
mensageiro	18. courier/messenger	bombeiro	24. firefighter	jornalista/repórter	30. journalist/ reporter
zelador	19. custodian/janitor	pescador	25. fisherman		
processador de dados	20. data processor	supervisor de fábrica	26. foreman		

[At a job interview]
A. Are you an experienced _____?
B. Yes. I'm a very experienced _____.

A. How long have you been a/an _____?
B. I've been a/an _____ for .... months/years.

Which of these occupations do you think are the most interesting? the most difficult? Why?

A. What's your occupation?
B. I'm a **lawyer**.
A. A **lawyer**?
B. Yes. That's right.

advogado	**1.** lawyer	farmacêutico	**6.** pharmacist	corretor de imóveis **11.** real estate agent
mecânico	**2.** mechanic	fotógrafo	**7.** photographer	recepcionista **12.** receptionist
modelo	**3.** model	piloto	**8.** pilot	reparador **13.** repairperson
apresentador de noticiário	**4.** newscaster	encanador	**9.** plumber	vendedor **14.** salesperson
pintor	**5.** painter	policial	**10.** police officer	lixeiro **15.** sanitation worker

cientista	**16.** scientist	alfaiate	**21.** tailor	motorista de caminhão	**26.** truck driver
costureira	**17.** seamstress	motorista de táxi	**22.** taxi driver	garçom	**27.** waiter
secretária	**18.** secretary	professora	**23.** teacher	garçonete	**28.** waitress
guarda de segurança	**19.** security guard	tradutora/intérprete	**24.** translator/interpreter	soldador	**29.** welder
estoquista	**20.** stock clerk	agente de viagens	**25.** travel agent	veterinário	**30.** veterinarian

A. Are you still a _____?
B. No. I'm a _____.
A. Oh. That's interesting.

A. What kind of job would you like in the future?
B. I'd like to be a _____.

Do you work? What's your occupation?
What are the occupations of people in your family?

ATIVIDADES PROFISSIONAIS

A. Can you **act**?
B. Yes, I can.

representar/atuar	**1.** act	
montar *aparelhos*	**2.** assemble	
eletrônicos	*components*	
assar	**3.** bake	
fazer/	**4.** build *things*/	
construir *coisas*	*construct things*	

fazer a faxina	**5.** clean
cozinhar	**6.** cook
entregar *pizzas*	**7.** deliver *pizzas*
projetar *prédios*	**8.** design *buildings*
desenhar	**9.** draw
dirigir *um caminhão*	**10.** drive *a truck*

arquivar	**11.** file
pilotar *um avião*	**12.** fly *an airplane*
cultivar *hortaliças*	**13.** grow *vegetables*
vigiar *prédios*	**14.** guard *buildings*

cortar *grama*	**15.** mow *lawns*	costurar	**22.** sew
operar *máquinas*	**16.** operate *equipment*	cantar	**23.** sing
pintar (paredes)	**17.** paint	ensinar	**24.** teach
tocar *piano*	**18.** play the *piano*	traduzir	**25.** translate
consertar *coisas*/fazer reparos	**19.** repair *things*/fix *things*	datilografar	**26.** type
vender *automóveis*	**20.** sell *cars*	lavar *pratos*	**27.** wash *dishes*
servir *refeições*	**21.** serve *food*	escrever/redigir	**28.** write

A. What do you do for a living?
B. I _____.

A. Do you know how to _____?
B. Yes. I've been _____ing for years.

Tell about your work abilities.
What can you do?

recepção	**1.** reception area	almoxarifado	**18.** supply room
chapeleira	**2.** coat rack	depósito	**19.** storage room
guarda-casacos	**3.** coat closet	sala de reuniões	**20.** conference room
quadro de avisos	**4.** message board	mesa de reuniões	**21.** conference table
escaninhos	**5.** mailbox	quadro/lousa (para caneta)	**22.** whiteboard/dry erase board
arquivo	**6.** file cabinet	sala dos funcionários	**23.** employee lounge
armário	**7.** supply cabinet	máquina de café	**24.** coffee machine
estante	**8.** storage cabinet	máquina de refrigerantes	**25.** soda machine
local de trabalho	**9.** workstation	recepcionista	**26.** receptionist
mesa com computador	**10.** computer workstation	datilógrafa/datilógrafo	**27.** typist
bebedouro	**11.** water cooler	arquivista	**28.** file clerk
carrinho de café	**12.** coffee cart	secretária	**29.** secretary
escritório/gabinete	**13.** office	assistente de administração	**30.** administrative assistant
expedição	**14.** mailroom	gerente	**31.** office manager
máquina franqueadora	**15.** postage machine/postage meter	auxiliar de escritório	**32.** office assistant
máquina de fotocópias	**16.** copier/(photo)copy machine	empregador/chefe/patrão	**33.** employer/boss
cesto de lixo	**17.** waste receptacle		

[1–25] A. Where's ....?
B ⎰ He's/She's in the/his/her _____.*
  ⎱ He's/She's at the/his/her _____.†
*1, 13, 14, 18–20, 23   †2–12, 15–17, 21, 22, 24, 25

[26–33] A. Who's he/she?
B. He's/She's the new _____.

EQUIPAMENTOS DE ESCRITÓRIO

A. Do you know how to work this **computer**?
B. No, I don't.
A. Let me show you how.

computador	**1.** computer	calculadora de mesa	**9.** adding machine
tela de computador	**2.** VDT/video display terminal	mini-gravador/ ditafone	**10.** microcassette recorder/ dictaphone
impressora (matricial)	**3.** (dot-matrix) printer	telefone	**11.** telephone
impressora (de tinta)	**4.** (letter-quality) printer	fones de ouvido	**12.** headset
impressora (a laser)	**5.** (laser) printer	central telefônica/ PBX	**13.** phone system
processador de textos	**6.** word processor	máquina de telex	**14.** telex machine
máquina de escrever		máquina de fax	**15.** fax machine
calculadora	**7.** typewriter	apontador	**16.** pencil sharpener
	8. calculator		

apontador elétrico	**17.** electric pencil sharpener
guilhotina para papel	**18.** paper cutter
máquina de encadernação	**19.** plastic binding machine
balança para cartas	**20.** postal scale
retalhadora de papel	**21.** paper shredder

A. I think this _____ is broken!
B. I'll take a look at it.

A. Have you seen the new _____?
B. No, I haven't.
A. It's much better than the old one!

Do you know how to operate a computer? a fax machine? Give step-by-step instructions for using some type of office equipment.

escrivaninha	**1.**	desk
cadeira giratória	**2.**	swivel chair
fichário giratório	**3.**	rolodex
porta-lápis	**4.**	pencil cup
caixa de correspondência	**5.**	letter tray/ stacking tray
porta-memorando	**6.**	memo holder
calendário de mesa	**7.**	desk calendar
abajur de mesa	**8.**	desk lamp
placa de nome	**9.**	nameplate
risque-rabisque	**10.**	desk pad
cesto de papel	**11.**	wastebasket
cadeira ergonômica	**12.**	posture chair/ clerical chair
calendário de parede	**13.**	wall calendar
agenda de parede	**14.**	wall planner
arquivo	**15.**	file cabinet
grampeador	**16.**	stapler
tira-grampos	**17.**	staple remover
porta-fita adesiva	**18.**	tape dispenser
porta-clipes	**19.**	paper clip dispenser
cartões de visita	**20.**	business cards
prancheta	**21.**	clipboard
agenda de mesa	**22.**	appointment book
agenda pessoal	**23.**	organizer/ personal planner
cartão de ponto	**24.**	timesheet
contracheque	**25.**	paycheck
abridor de cartas	**26.**	letter opener
tesoura	**27.**	scissors
furador	**28.**	punch
furador de 3 buracos	**29.**	3-hole punch
almofada/berço	**30.**	stamp pad/ink pad
carimbo	**31.**	rubber stamp
caneta	**32.**	pen
lápis	**33.**	pencil
lapiseira	**34.**	mechanical pencil
marcador de texto	**35.**	highlighter (pen)
borracha	**36.**	eraser

[1–15]
A. Welcome to the company.
B. Thank you.
A. How do you like your _____?
B. It's/They're very nice.

[16–36]
A. My desk is such a mess! I can't find my _____!
B. Here it is/Here they are next to your _____.

Which items on this page do you have? Do you have an appointment book, personal planner, or calendar? How do you remember important things such as appointments, meetings, and birthdays?

MATERIAL DE ESCRITÓRIO

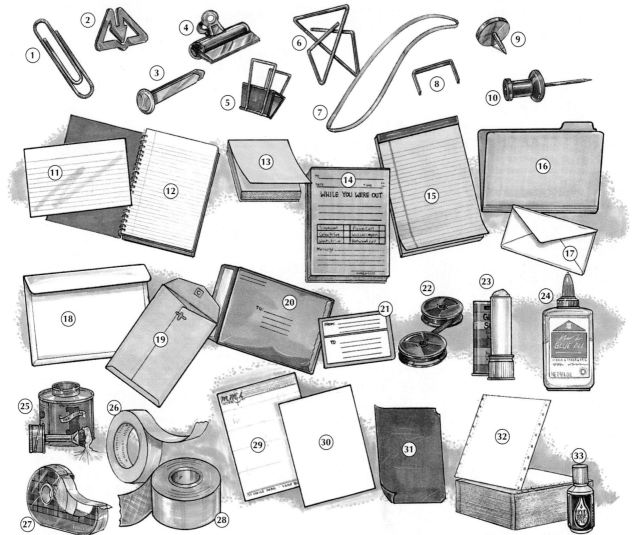

clipe	**1.** paper clip	bloco pautado	**15.** legal pad
clipe de plástico	**2.** plastic clip	pasta de arquivo	**16.** file folder/
colchete de arquivo	**3.** paper fastener		manila folder
grampo de mola	**4.** bulldog clip	envelope	**17.** envelope
grampo de pressão	**5.** binder clip	envelope para	**18.** catalog envelope
grampo/clipão	**6.** clamp	catálogos	
elástico	**7.** rubber band	envelope com	**19.** clasp envelope
grampo	**8.** staple	fecho de metal	
tachinha	**9.** thumbtack	envelope de correio	**20.** mailer
alfinete marcador	**10.** pushpin	etiqueta de endereço	**21.** mailing label
ficha de arquivo	**11.** index card	fita para máquina	**22.** typewriter ribbon
caderno	**12.** memo pad/	de escrever	
	note pad	bastão de cola	**23.** gluestick
bloco Post-It	**13.** Post-It note pad	cola branca	**24.** glue
bloco para recados	**14.** message pad	cola pastosa	**25.** rubber cement

fita crepe	**26.** masking tape		
fita adesiva	**27.** Scotch tape/		
transparente	cellophane tape		
fita adesiva para	**28.** sealing tape/		
empacotamento	package mailing		
	tape		
papel timbrado	**29.** stationery		
papel para máquina	**30.** typing paper		
de escrever			
papel carbono	**31.** carbon paper		
papel para	**32.** computer paper		
computador			
líquido corretor	**33.** correction fluid		

A. {
We've run out of [1–23] s.
We've run out of [24–33] .
}

B. I'll get some more from the supply room.

A. Could I borrow a/an/some [1–33] ?

B. Sure. Here you are.

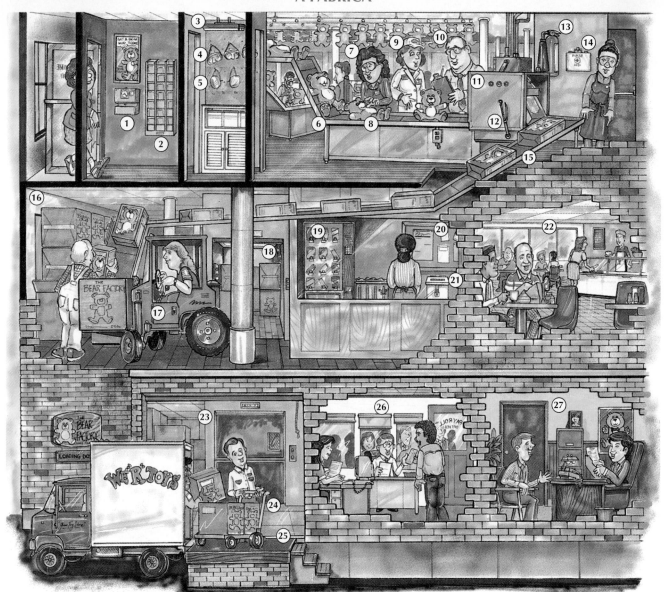

relógio de ponto	**1.** time clock	supervisor	**10.** foreman	vendedora automática	**19.** vending machine
cartões de ponto	**2.** time cards	máquina	**11.** machine	aviso sindical	**20.** union notice
almoxarifado	**3.** supply room	alavanca	**12.** lever	caixa de sugestões	**21.** suggestion box
óculos de segurança	**4.** safety glasses	extintor de incêndio	**13.** fire extinguisher	cantina/lanchonete	**22.** cafeteria
máscaras	**5.** masks	kit de primeiros	**14.** first-aid kit	setor de expedição	**23.** shipping
linha de montagem	**6.** (assembly) line	socorros			department
operário	**7.** worker	esteira	**15.** conveyor belt	carrinho de carga	**24.** hand truck
local de trabalho	**8.** work station	armazém/depósito	**16.** warehouse	plataforma de	**25.** loading dock
supervisor de con-	**9.** quality control	empilhadeira	**17.** forklift	carregamento	
trole de qualidade	supervisor	elevador de carga	**18.** freight elevator	seção de pagamento	**26.** payroll office
				seção de pessoal	**27.** personnel office

A. Excuse me. I'm a new employee.
    Where's/Where are the _____?
B. Next to/Near/In/On the _____.

A. Have you seen *Fred*?
B. Yes. He's in/on/at/next to/near
    the _____.

Are there any factories where you live? What kind?
What are the working conditions there?

What products do factories in your country produce?

carrinho de mão	**1.** wheelbarrow	nível de bolha	**11.** level	furgão	**22.** van
porta-ferramentas	**2.** toolbelt	escada	**12.** ladder	escavadora	**23.** backhoe
pá	**3.** shovel	andaime	**13.** scaffolding	cimento	**24.** cement
marreta	**4.** sledgehammer	caminhão basculante	**14.** dump truck	madeira	**25.** wood/lumber
picareta	**5.** pickax	trator carregador	**15.** front-end loader	madeira compensada	**26.** plywood
britadeira	**6.** jackhammer/	máquina de terraplenagem	**16.** bulldozer	arame/fio	**27.** wire
	pneumatic drill	grua/guindaste	**17.** cherry picker	fibra de isolamento	**28.** insulation
capacete	**7.** helmet/hard hat	guindaste	**18.** crane	tijolo	**29.** brick
plantas	**8.** blueprints	betoneira	**19.** cement mixer	telha de madeira	**30.** shingle
colher de pedreiro	**9.** trowel	picape/caminhonete	**20.** pickup truck	tubo	**31.** pipe
trena	**10.** tape measure	trailer	**21.** trailer	viga de ferro	**32.** girder/beam

[1–12]
A. Could you get me that/those _____?
B. Sure.

[13–23]
A. Watch out for that _____!
B. Oh! Thanks for the warning!

[24–32]
A. Are we going to have enough [24–28] / [29–32] s to finish the job?
B. I think so.

farol	**1.** headlight	porta-malas	**16.** trunk	filtro de ar	**32.** air filter
pára-choque	**2.** bumper	lanterna traseira	**17.** taillight	bateria	**33.** battery
seta	**3.** turn signal	luz de freio	**18.** brake light	medidor de óleo	**34.** dipstick
lanterna	**4.** parking light	farol de ré	**19.** backup light	alternador	**35.** alternator
pneu	**5.** tire	placa de registro	**20.** license plate	radiador	**36.** radiator
calota	**6.** hubcap	escapamento	**21.** tailpipe	correia	**37.** fan belt
capô	**7.** hood	silenciador	**22.** muffler	mangueira do radiador	**38.** radiator hose
pára-brisa	**8.** windshield	transmissão	**23.** transmission	posto (de gasolina/de	**39.** gas station/
limpador do	**9.** windshield	tanque de combustível	**24.** gas tank	serviço)	service station
pára-brisa	wipers	macaco	**25.** jack	bomba de ar	**40.** air pump
retrovisor lateral	**10.** side mirror	estepe	**26.** spare tire	área de manutenção	**41.** service bay
antena	**11.** antenna	sinalizador de	**27.** flare	mecânico	**42.** mechanic
teto solar	**12.** sunroof	emergência		frentista	**43.** attendant
bagageiro	**13.** luggage rack/	cabos de ligação direta	**28.** jumper cables	bomba de combustível	**44.** gas pump
	luggage carrier	motor	**29.** engine	bocal (da bomba)	**45.** nozzle
pára-brisa traseiro	**14.** rear windshield	velas de ignição	**30.** spark plugs		
desembaçador traseiro	**15.** rear defroster	carburador	**31.** carburetor		

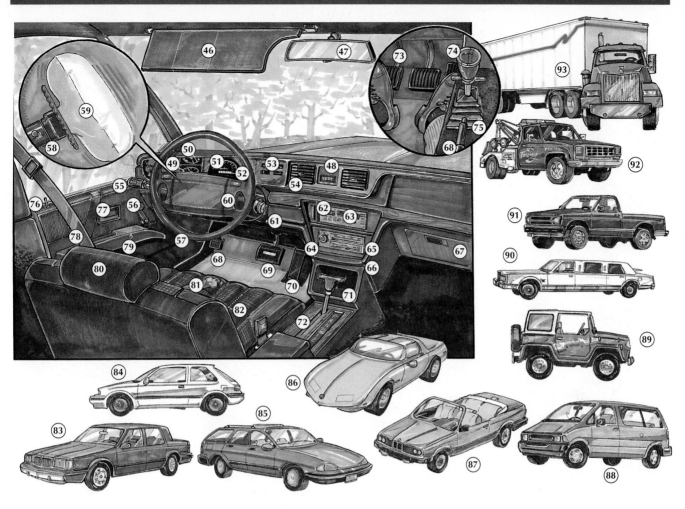

quebra-sol	**46.** visor	rádio	**62.** radio	trava da porta	**76.** door lock
espelho retrovisor	**47.** rearview mirror	toca-fitas	**63.** tape deck/	maçaneta da porta	**77.** door handle
painel	**48.** dashboard/		cassette player	cinto de segurança	**78.** shoulder harness
	instrument panel	condicionador de ar	**64.** air conditioning	apoio para braço	**79.** armrest
indicador de	**49.** gas gauge/	aquecedor	**65.** heater	apoio para pescoço	**80.** headrest
combustível	fuel gauge	desembaçador	**66.** defroster	cinto de segurança	**81.** seat belt
indicador de	**50.** temperature gauge	porta-luvas	**67.** glove	assento	**82.** seat
temperatura			compartment	sedã	**83.** sedan
velocímetro	**51.** speedometer	freio de mão	**68.** emergency brake	carro de três portas	**84.** hatchback
hodômetro	**52.** odometer	freio	**69.** brake	perua	**85.** station wagon
pisca alerta	**53.** warning lights	acelerador	**70.** accelerator/	carro-esporte	**86.** sports car
ventilador	**54.** vent		gas pedal	conversível	**87.** convertible
seta	**55.** turn signal	câmbio automático	**71.** gearshift	furgonete/perua/kombi	**88.** minivan
piloto automático	**56.** cruise control	transmissão automática	**72.** automatic	jipe	**89.** jeep
volante/direção	**57.** steering wheel		transmission	limusine	**90.** limousine
coluna da direção	**58.** steering column	embreagem	**73.** clutch	picape/caminhonete	**91.** pick-up truck
air bag	**59.** air bag	câmbio manual	**74.** stickshift	guincho	**92.** tow truck
buzina	**60.** horn	transmissão manual	**75.** manual	caminhão	**93.** truck
ignição	**61.** ignition		transmission		

[1, 3, 8–15, 23, 34–38, 46–82]
A. What's the matter with your car?
B. The _____(s) is/are broken.

[1, 4–6, 9–11, 30–33, 37, 38]
A. Can I help you?
B. Yes. I need to replace a/the _____(s).

[1, 2, 4–8, 10–14, 16–20]
A. I was just in a car accident!
B. Oh, no! Were you hurt?
A. No. But my _____(s) was/were damaged.

túnel	**1.** tunnel	pista da esquerda	**14.** left lane	via de sentido único	**27.** one-way street
ponte	**2.** bridge	pista do meio	**15.** middle lane/	faixa amarela dupla	**28.** double yellow line
posto de pedágio	**3.** tollbooth		center lane	travessia de pedestres	**29.** crosswalk
pista de cobrança	**4.** exact change lane	pista da direita	**16.** right lane	cruzamento	**30.** intersection
automática		acostamento	**17.** shoulder	travessia escolar	**31.** school crossing
sinalização viária	**5.** route sign	faixa intermitente	**18.** broken line	esquina	**32.** corner
auto-estrada/rodovia	**6.** highway	faixa contínua	**19.** solid line	semáforo/sinal	**33.** traffic light
estrada	**7.** road	sinal de limite de	**20.** speed limit sign	sinal de proibido	**34.** no left turn sign
barreira	**8.** divider/barrier	velocidade		virar à esquerda	
viaduto	**9.** overpass	(rampa de) saída	**21.** exit (ramp)	sinal de proibido	**35.** no right turn sign
passagem inferior	**10.** underpass	sinal/aviso de saída	**22.** exit sign	virar à direita	
(rampa de) entrada	**11.** entrance ramp/	sinal de via preferencial	**23.** yield sign	sinal de	**36.** no U-turn sign
	on ramp	posto de serviço	**24.** service area	retorno proibido	
auto-estrada	**12.** interstate (highway)	cruzamento de	**25.** railroad crossing	sinal de entrada	**37.** do not enter sign
interestadual/rodovia		via férrea		proibida	
canteiro central	**13.** median	rua	**26.** street	sinal de pare	**38.** stop sign

A. Where's the
    accident?
B. It's on/in/at/near
    the _____.

Describe a highway you travel on.   In your area, on which highways and streets do most
Describe an intersection near where you live.   accidents occur? Why are these places dangerous?

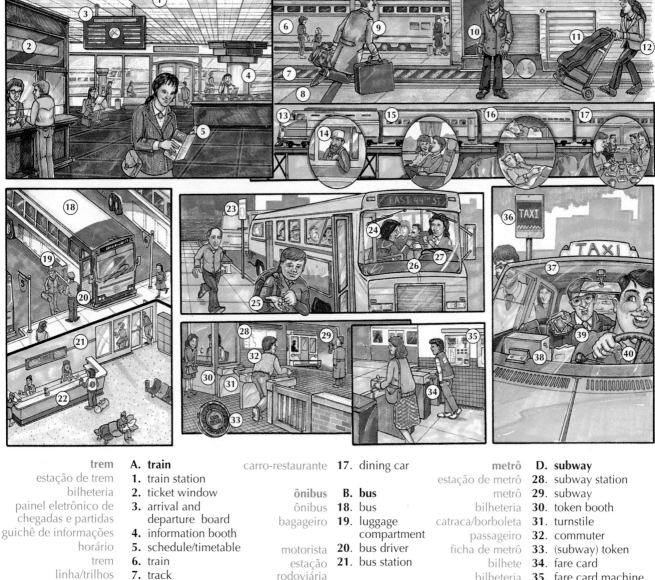

trem	**A. train**	carro-restaurante	17. dining car	metrô **D. subway**
estação de trem	1. train station			estação de metrô 28. subway station
bilheteria	2. ticket window	ônibus	**B. bus**	metrô 29. subway
painel eletrônico de	3. arrival and	ônibus	18. bus	bilheteria 30. token booth
chegadas e partidas	departure board	bagageiro	19. luggage	catraca/borboleta 31. turnstile
guichê de informações	4. information booth		compartment	passageiro 32. commuter
horário	5. schedule/timetable	motorista	20. bus driver	ficha de metrô 33. (subway) token
trem	6. train	estação	21. bus station	bilhete 34. fare card
linha/trilhos	7. track	rodoviária		bilheteria 35. fare card machine
plataforma	8. platform	bilheteria	22. ticket counter	automática
passageiro	9. passenger			
chefe de trem	10. conductor	ônibus local	**C. local bus**	táxi **E. taxi**
bagagem	11. luggage/baggage	ponto de ônibus	23. bus stop	ponto de táxi 36. taxi stand
carregador	12. porter/redcap	passageiro	24. rider/passenger	táxi 37. taxi/cab/taxicab
máquina/locomotiva	13. engine	tarifa	25. (bus) fare	taxímetro 38. meter
maquinista	14. engineer	caixa	26. fare box	tarifa 39. fare
vagão de passageiros	15. passenger car	bilhete de	27. transfer	motorista de táxi 40. cab driver/taxi driver
vagão-leito/	16. sleeper	integração		
carro dormitório				

[A–E]

A. How are you going to get there?

B. { I'm going to take the [A–D] .
{ I'm going to take a [E] .

[1–8, 10–23, 26, 28–31, 35, 36]

A. Excuse me. Where's the _____?

B. Over there.

O AEROPORTO

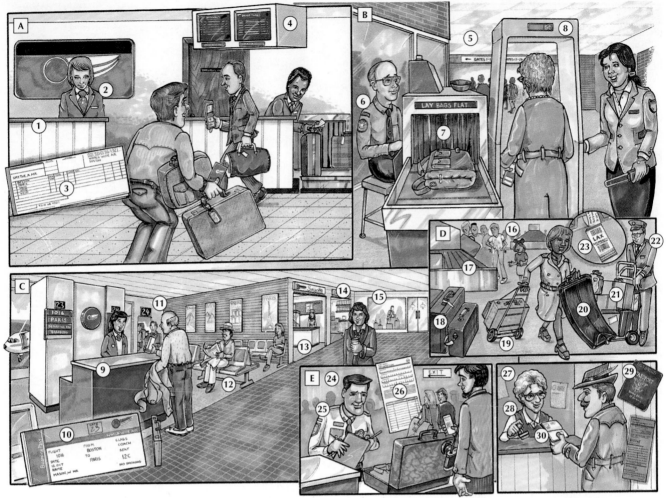

Check-In	A. Check-In
balcão/guichê	1. ticket counter
funcionário/funcionária	2. ticket agent
passagem/bilhete	3. ticket
painel eletrônico	4. arrival and departure monitor

Segurança	B. Security
barreira de segurança	5. security checkpoint
guarda de segurança	6. security guard
máquina de raio-X	7. X-ray machine
detetor de metais	8. metal detector

Portão de Embarque	C. The Gate
balcão	9. check-in counter
cartão de embarque	10. boarding pass
portão de embarque	11. gate
salão de embarque/espera	12. waiting area
bar	13. concession stand/snack bar
loja de presentes	14. gift shop
freeshop	15. duty-free shop

Retirada de Bagagem	D. Baggage Claim
área de retirada de bagagem	16. baggage claim (area)
carrossel de bagagem	17. baggage carousel
mala	18. suitcase
carrinho de mala	19. luggage carrier
porta-terno	20. garment bag
bagagem	21. baggage
carregador	22. porter/skycap
talão de registro de malas	23. (baggage) claim check

Alfândega e Imigração	E. Customs and Immigration
alfândega	24. customs
oficial da alfândega	25. customs officer
formulário da alfândega	26. customs declaration form
balcão de imigração/balcão de controle de passaportes	27. immigration
oficial de imigração	28. immigration officer
passaporte	29. passport
visto	30. visa

[1, 2, 4–9, 11–17, 24, 25, 27, 28]

A. Excuse me. Where's the _____?*

B. Right over there.

*With 24 and 27, use: Excuse me. Where's _____?

[3, 10, 18–21, 23, 26, 29, 30]

A. Oh, no! I think I've lost my _____!

B. I'll help you look for it.

cabina	**1.** cockpit
piloto/capitão	**2.** pilot/captain
co-piloto	**3.** co-pilot
painel de instrumentos	**4.** instrument panel
engenheiro de vôo	**5.** flight engineer
cabine de primeira-classe	**6.** first-class section
passageiro	**7.** passenger
cozinha	**8.** galley
comissário(a) de bordo	**9.** flight attendant
toalete/banheiro	**10.** lavatory/bathroom
cabine de passageiros	**11.** cabin
maleta de mão	**12.** carry-on bag
bagageiro	**13.** overhead compartment
corredor	**14.** aisle
cinto de segurança	**15.** seat belt
assento da janela	**16.** window seat
assento do meio	**17.** middle seat
assento do corredor	**18.** aisle seat
luminoso de 'apertar cintos'	**19.** Fasten Seat Belt sign
luminoso de 'proibido fumar'	**20.** No Smoking sign
botão de chamada	**21.** call button
máscara de oxigênio	**22.** oxygen mask
saída de emergência	**23.** emergency exit
apoio para braço	**24.** armrest

botão de assento	**25.** seat control
mesa	**26.** tray (table)
refeição	**27.** meal
bolso do assento	**28.** seat pocket
cartão de instruções de emergência	**29.** emergency instruction card
saco para enjôo	**30.** air sickness bag
colete inflável	**31.** life vest
pista de pouso/decolagem	**32.** runway
terminal	**33.** terminal (building)
torre de controle	**34.** control tower
avião/aeronave/jato	**35.** airplane/plane/jet
nariz/proa	**36.** nose
fuselagem	**37.** fuselage
porta de carga	**38.** cargo door
trem de pouso	**39.** landing gear
asa	**40.** wing
motor	**41.** engine
cauda	**42.** tail
avião turboélice	**43.** propeller plane/prop
hélice	**44.** propeller
helicóptero	**45.** helicopter
lâmina do rotor	**46.** rotor (blade)

A. Where's the _____?

B. In/On/Next to/Behind/In front of/Above/ Below the _____.

Ladies and gentlemen. This is your captain speaking. I'm sorry for the delay. We had a little problem with one of our _____s.* Everything is fine now and we'll be taking off shortly.

*Use 4, 7, 10, 12, 20–22, 24.

O Tempo	A. Weather				
ensolarado	1. sunny	caindo neve com chuva	12. sleeting	muito quente/ muito calor	21. hot
nublado	2. cloudy	relâmpago	13. lightning	quente/calor	22. warm
claro	3. clear	tempestade	14. thunderstorm	fresco	23. cool
nebuloso	4. hazy	nevasca	15. snowstorm	frio	24. cold
enevoado	5. foggy	furacão	16. hurricane/typhoon	muito frio	25. freezing
ventoso	6. windy	tornado/ciclone	17. tornado		
úmido/abafado	7. humid/muggy			As Estações	C. Seasons
chovendo	8. raining	Temperatura	B. Temperature	verão	26. summer
garoando	9. drizzling	termômetro	18. thermometer	outono	27. fall/autumn
nevando	10. snowing	Fahrenheit	19. Fahrenheit	inverno	28. winter
chovendo granizo	11. hailing	centígrado	20. Centigrade/Celsius	primavera	29. spring

[1–12]
A. What's the weather like?
B. It's _____.

[13–17]
A. What's the weather forecast?
B. There's going to be
   _[13]_ /a _[14–17]_ .

[19–25]
A. How's the weather?
B. It's _[21–25]_ .
A. What's the temperature?
B. It's ……. degrees _[19, 20]_ .

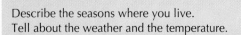

Describe the seasons where you live.
Tell about the weather and the temperature.

What's your favorite season?
Why?

acampar	A. camping
barraca	1. tent
mochila	2. backpack
saco de dormir	3. sleeping bag
estacas de barraca	4. tent stakes
machado	5. hatchet
lampião/lanterna	6. lantern
fogão de acampamento	7. camp stove

caminhar	B. hiking
botas de caminhar	8. hiking boots
bússola	9. compass
mapa de trilhas	10. trail map

fazer montanhismo	C. mountain climbing
botas de caminhar	11. hiking boots

fazer alpinismo	D. rock climbing
corda	12. rope
arreio de segurança	13. harness

piquenique	E. picnic
pano/esteira	14. (picnic) blanket
garrafa térmica	15. thermos
cesta de piquenique	16. picnic basket

[A–E]
A. Let's go _____* this weekend.
B. Good idea! We haven't gone _____* in a long time.

*With E, say: on a picnic

[1–16]
A. Did you bring the _____?
B. Yes, I did.

Have you ever gone camping or hiking?
Where? What equipment did you use?

Do you like to go on picnics? Where?
What picnic supplies and food do you take with you?

pista de cooper	1.	jogging path
banheiros	2.	rest rooms
estátua	3.	statue
área de piqueniques	4.	picnic area
mesa de piquenique	5.	picnic table
churrasqueira	6.	grill
lata de lixo	7.	trash can
carrossel/gira-gira	8.	merry-go-round/carousel
fonte	9.	fountain
zoológico	10.	zoo
bebedouro	11.	water fountain
concha acústica	12.	band shell
trilha de cavalo	13.	bridle path
bicicletário	14.	bike rack
lago de patos	15.	duck pond
pista de bicicletas	16.	bicycle path/bikeway
banco	17.	bench
playground	18.	playground
estrutura para escalar	19.	jungle gym
barras fixas	20.	monkey bars
escorregador	21.	slide
balanços	22.	swings
balanço de pneu	23.	tire swing
gangorra	24.	seesaw
piscina infantil	25.	wading pool
caixa de areia	26.	sandbox
areia	27.	sand

[1–18] A. Excuse me. Does this park have (a) _____?
B. Yes. Right over there.

[19–27] A. { Be careful on the __[19–24]__ !
Be careful in the __[25–27]__ !
B. I will, Mom/Dad.

Describe a park and a playground you are familiar with.

salva-vidas	**1.** lifeguard	pessoa tomando	**11.** sunbather	pipa	**21.** kite
posto do salva-vidas	**2.** lifeguard stand	banho de sol		colchão de ar	**22.** raft/air mattress
bóia de salvamento	**3.** life preserver	castelo de areia	**12.** sand castle	bóia	**23.** tube
bar/lanchonete	**4.** snack bar/	concha	**13.** seashell/shell	pano/esteira	**24.** (beach) blanket
	refreshment stand	pára-sol/guarda-sol	**14.** beach umbrella	chapéu de sol	**25.** sun hat
duna de areia	**5.** sand dune	cadeira (de praia)	**15.** (beach) chair	óculos de sol	**26.** sunglasses
rocha	**6.** rock	toalha (de praia)	**16.** (beach) towel	bronzeador	**27.** suntan lotion/
banhista	**7.** swimmer	maiô	**17.** bathing suit/		sunscreen
onda	**8.** wave		swimsuit	balde	**28.** pail/bucket
surfista	**9.** surfer	touca	**18.** bathing cap	pá	**29.** shovel
vendedor	**10.** vendor	pranchinha	**19.** kickboard	bola de praia	**30.** beach ball
ambulante		prancha de surfe	**20.** surfboard	isopor	**31.** cooler

[1–13]
A. What a nice beach!
B. It is. Look at all the _____s!

[14–31]
A. Are you ready for the beach?
B. Almost. I just have to get my _____.

Do you like to go to the beach? Describe your favorite beach. What do you take when you go there?

ESPORTES E ATIVIDADES RECREATIVAS INDIVIDUAIS

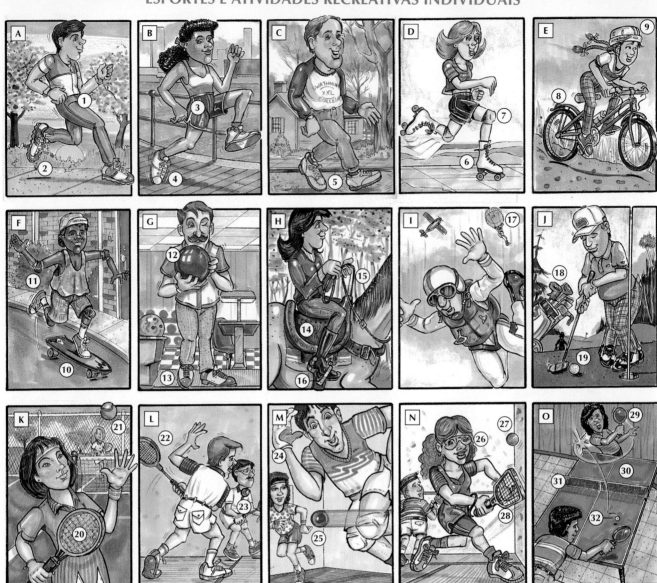

fazer cooper	**A. jogging**	jogar boliche	**G. bowling**	squash	**L. squash**
agasalho/training	**1.** jogging suit	bola de boliche	**12.** bowling ball	raquete de squash	**22.** squash racquet
tênis de cooper	**2.** jogging shoes	sapatos de boliche	**13.** bowling shoes	bola de squash	**23.** squash ball

correr	**B. running**	andar a cavalo	**H. horseback riding**	handball	**M. handball**
calção de correr	**3.** running shorts	sela	**14.** saddle	luva de handball	**24.** handball glove
tênis de correr	**4.** running shoes	arreio	**15.** reins	bola de handball	**25.** handball
		estribos	**16.** stirrups		

andar a pé	**C. walking**			racquetball	**N. racquetball**
tênis	**5.** walking shoes	vôo livre	**I. skydiving**	óculos de proteção	**26.** safety goggles
		pára-quedas	**17.** parachute	bola de racquetball	**27.** racquetball
				raquete	**28.** racquet

patinar	**D. roller skating**	golfe	**J. golf**		
patins	**6.** roller skates	tacos de golfe	**18.** golf clubs	pingue-pongue	**O. ping pong**
joelheiras	**7.** knee pads	bola de golfe	**19.** golf ball	raquete de pingue-pongue	**29.** paddle

andar de bicicleta	**E. cycling/**			mesa de pingue-pongue	**30.** ping pong table
fazer ciclismo	**bicycling/biking**	tênis	**K. tennis**	rede	**31.** net
bicicleta	**8.** bicycle/bike	raquete de tênis	**20.** tennis racquet	bola de pingue-pongue	**32.** ping pong ball
capacete	**9.** (bicycle) helmet	bola de tênis	**21.** tennis ball		

andar de skate	**F. skateboarding**
skate	**10.** skateboard
cotoveleiras	**11.** elbow pads

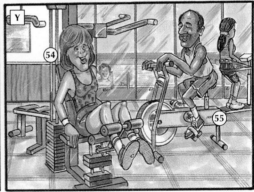

disco frisbee	**P.**	**frisbee**
disco frisbee	**33.**	frisbee
dardos	**Q.**	**darts**
alvo	**34.**	dartboard
dardos	**35.**	darts
bilhar	**R.**	**billiards/pool**
mesa de bilhar	**36.**	pool table
bolas de bilhar	**37.**	billiard balls
taco de bilhar	**38.**	pool stick
karatê	**S.**	**karate**
uniforme de karatê	**39.**	karate outfit
faixa de karatê	**40.**	karate belt

ginástica olímpica	**T.**	**gymnastics**
barra fixa	**41.**	balance beam
paralelas	**42.**	parallel bars
capacho/esteira	**43.**	mat
cavalo-de-pau	**44.**	horse
cama elástica	**45.**	trampoline
halterofilismo	**U.**	**weightlifting**
halteres	**46.**	barbell
pesos	**47.**	weights
arco e flecha	**V.**	**archery**
arco e flecha	**48.**	bow and arrow
alvo	**49.**	target

lutar boxe	**W.**	**box**
luvas de boxe	**50.**	boxing gloves
calção de boxe	**51.**	(boxing) trunks
fazer luta livre	**X.**	**wrestle**
uniforme de luta livre	**52.**	wrestling uniform
lona/esteira de luta livre	**53.**	(wrestling) mat
fazer ginástica	**Y.**	**work out**
equipamentos de ginástica	**54.**	universal/exercise equipment
bicicleta ergométrica	**55.**	exercise bike

[A–Y]

A. What do you like to do in your free time?

B. {
I like to go [A–I].
I like to play [J–R].
I like to do [S–V].
I like to [W–Y].

[1–55]

A. I really like this/these new _____.

B. It's/They're very nice.

ESPORTES DE EQUIPE

[A–H]
A. Do you like **baseball**?
B. Yes. **Baseball** is one of my favorite sports.

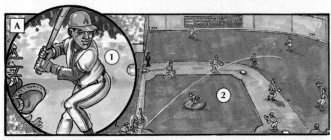

beisebol	**A. baseball**	hóquei no gelo	**E. (ice) hockey**
jogador de beisebol	**1.** baseball player	jogador de hóquei	**9.** hockey player
campo de beisebol	**2.** baseball field/ballfield	pista/ringue de hóquei	**10.** hockey rink
softball	**B. softball**	basquete	**F. basketball**
jogador de softball	**3.** softball player	jogador de basquete	**11.** basketball player
campo	**4.** ballfield	quadra de basquete	**12.** basketball court
futebol americano	**C. football**	vôlei	**G. volleyball**
jogador de futebol americano	**5.** football player	jogador/jogadora de vôlei	**13.** volleyball player
campo de futebol americano	**6.** football field	quadra de vôlei	**14.** volleyball court
lacrosse	**D. lacrosse**	futebol	**H. soccer**
jogador de lacrosse	**7.** lacrosse player	jogador de futebol	**15.** soccer player
campo de lacrosse	**8.** lacrosse field	campo de futebol	**16.** soccer field

A. .... plays [A–H] very well.
B. You're right. I think he's/she's one
of the best _____s* on the team.

*Use 1, 3, 5, 7, 9, 11, 13, 15.

A. Now, listen! I want all of you
to go out on that _____† and
play the best game of [A–H]
you've ever played!
B. All right, Coach!

†Use 2, 4, 6, 8, 10, 12, 14, 16.

Which sports on this page do you like
to play? Which do you like to
watch?
What are your favorite teams?
Name some famous players of these
sports.

[1–27]
A. I can't find my **baseball**!
B. Look in the *closet*.*

*closet, basement, garage

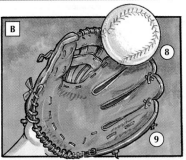

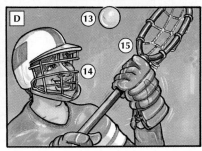

beisebol	**A.**	**baseball**
bola de beisebol	**1.**	baseball
taco	**2.**	bat
capacete de batedor	**3.**	batting helmet
uniforme de beisebol	**4.**	baseball uniform
máscara protetora de apanhador	**5.**	catcher's mask
luva de beisebol	**6.**	baseball glove
luva de apanhador	**7.**	catcher's mitt
softball	**B.**	**softball**
bola de softball	**8.**	softball
luva de softball	**9.**	softball glove

futebol americano	**C.**	**football**
bola	**10.**	football
capacete	**11.**	football helmet
ombreiras	**12.**	shoulder pads
lacrosse	**D.**	**lacrosse**
bola de lacrosse	**13.**	lacrosse ball
protetor de rosto	**14.**	face guard
raquete de lacrosse	**15.**	lacrosse stick
hóquei (no gelo)	**E.**	**hockey**
disco de hóquei	**16.**	hockey puck
taco de hóquei	**17.**	hockey stick
máscara de hóquei	**18.**	hockey mask
luva de hóquei	**19.**	hockey glove
patins de hóquei	**20.**	hockey skates

basquete	**F.**	**basketball**
bola de basquete	**21.**	basketball
tabela	**22.**	backboard
rede	**23.**	basketball hoop
vôlei	**G.**	**volleyball**
bola de vôlei	**24.**	volleyball
rede de vôlei	**25.**	volleyball net
futebol	**H.**	**soccer**
bola de futebol	**26.**	soccer ball
caneleiras	**27.**	shinguards

[In a store]
A. Excuse me. I'm looking for
(a) [1–27].
B. All our [A–H] equipment is over there.
A. Thanks.

[At home]
A. I'm going to play [A–H] after school today.
B. Don't forget your [1–21, 24–27]!

Which sports on this page are popular in your country? Which sports are played in high school?

ESPORTES E ATIVIDADES RECREATIVAS DE INVERNO

[A–H]
A. What's your favorite winter sport?
B. **Skiing**.

esquiar (em pistas/rampas)	**A. (downhill) skiing**	dança/balé no gelo	**D. figure skating**
esquis	**1.** skis	patins para balé no gelo	**8.** figure skates
botas de esquiar	**2.** ski boots	andar de trenó	**E. sledding**
trava-botas/atacas	**3.** bindings	trenó	**9.** sled
bastões	**4.** poles	trenó circular	**10.** sledding dish/saucer
esquiar (fora de pistas)	**B. cross-country skiing**	andar em tobogã olímpico	**F. bobsledding**
esquis especiais (para fora de pistas)	**5.** cross-country skis	tobogã olímpico	**11.** bobs led
patinação (no gelo)	**C. (ice) skating**	andar em trenó motorizado	**G. snowmobiling**
patins (de gelo)	**6.** (ice) skates	trenó motorizado	**12.** snowmobile
protetores de patins	**7.** skate guards	andar de tobogã	**H. tobogganing**
		tobogã	**13.** toboggan

[A–H]
   [At work or at school on Friday]
A. What are you going to do this
   weekend?
B. I'm going to go _____.

[1–13]
   [On the telephone]
A. Hello. Jimmy's Sporting Goods.
B. Hello. Do you sell _____(s)?
A. Yes, we do./No, we don't.

Have you ever watched the Winter
Olympics? What is your favorite
event? Which event do you think
is the most exciting? the most
dangerous?

[A–L]
A. Would you like to go **sailing** tomorrow?
B. Sure. I'd love to.

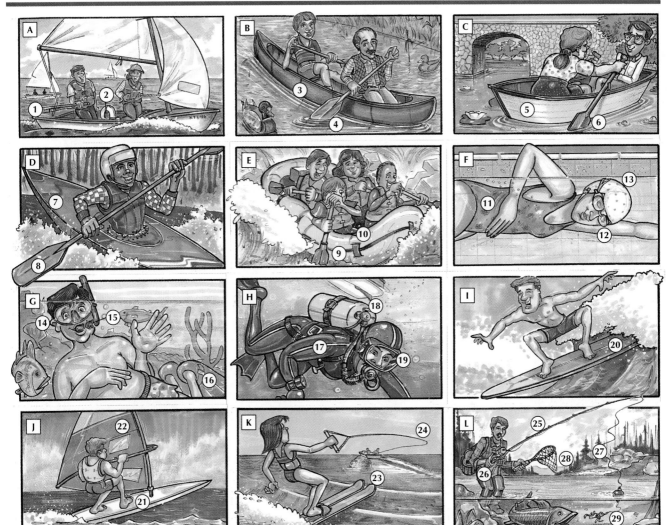

velejar	**A.**	**sailing**
barco a vela	**1.**	sailboat
salva-vidas	**2.**	life preserver
andar de canoa	**B.**	**canoeing**
canoa	**3.**	canoe
remos	**4.**	paddles
remar	**C.**	**rowing**
barco a remo	**5.**	rowboat
remos	**6.**	oars
andar de caiaque	**D.**	**kayaking**
caiaque	**7.**	kayak
remo	**8.**	paddle
remar em barco inflável (em correntezas fortes)	**E.**	**(white water) rafting**

barco inflável	**9.**	raft
colete salvavidas	**10.**	life jacket
nadar	**F.**	**swimming**
maiô/roupa de banho	**11.**	swimsuit/ bathing suit
óculos de nadar	**12.**	goggles
touca	**13.**	bathing cap
mergulho livre	**G.**	**snorkeling**
máscara (de mergulho)	**14.**	mask
tubo de respiração	**15.**	snorkel
pé de pato	**16.**	flippers
mergulho autônomo	**H.**	**scuba diving**
roupa de mergulho	**17.**	wet suit
tubo de ar	**18.**	(air) tank
máscara de mergulho	**19.**	(diving) mask

surfar	**I.**	**surfing**
prancha de surfe	**20.**	surfboard
fazer windsurfe	**J.**	**windsurfing**
prancha de windsurfe	**21.**	sailboard
vela	**22.**	sail
fazer esqui aquático	**K.**	**waterskiing**
esquis aquático	**23.**	water skis
corda	**24.**	towrope
pescar	**L.**	**fishing**
vara de pescar	**25.**	(fishing) rod
carretilha	**26.**	reel
linha	**27.**	(fishing) line
rede	**28.**	net
isca	**29.**	bait

bater	**1.** hit	caminhar	**13.** walk	levantar	**25.** lift
arremessar	**2.** pitch	correr	**14.** run	nadar	**26.** swim
jogar	**3.** throw	pular num só pé	**15.** hop	mergulhar	**27.** dive
pegar	**4.** catch	pular	**16.** skip	atirar	**28.** shoot
passar	**5.** pass	saltar	**17.** jump	flexão de braços	**29.** push-up
chutar	**6.** kick	ajoelhar	**18.** kneel	abdominais (sentado)	**30.** sit-up
sacar	**7.** serve	sentar	**19.** sit	levantar as pernas	**31.** leg lift
quicar	**8.** bounce	deitar	**20.** lie down	polichinelo	**32.** jumping jack
driblar	**9.** dribble	esticar	**21.** reach	flexão de joelhos	**33.** deep knee bend
atirar	**10.** shoot	girar	**22.** swing	dar cambalhota	**34.** somersault
fazer alongamento	**11.** stretch	empurrar	**23.** push	fazer estrela	**35.** cartwheel
fazer flexão	**12.** bend	puxar	**24.** pull	plantar bananeira	**36.** handstand

[1–10] A. _____ the ball!
B. Okay, Coach!

[11–28] A. Now _____!
B. Like this?
A. Yes.

[29–36] A. Okay, everybody. I want you to do twenty _____s!
B. Twenty _____s?!
A. That's right.

Do you exercise regularly?
Which exercises do you do?

Be an exercise instructor. Lead your friends in an exercise routine using the actions on this page.

[A–Q]
A. What's your hobby?
B. **Sewing.**

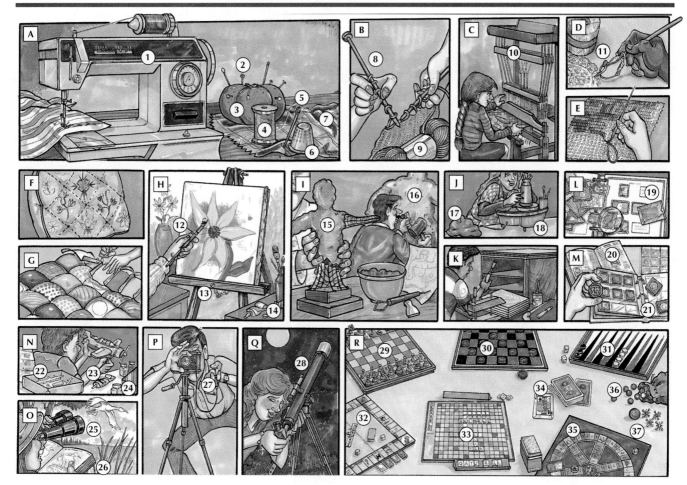

costura	**A. sewing**	**pintura**	**H. painting**	cola de modelismo	**23.** (model) glue

costura	**A. sewing**	**pintura**	**H. painting**
máquina de costura	**1.** sewing machine	pincel	**12.** paintbrush
alfinete	**2.** pin	cavalete	**13.** easel
alfineteira	**3.** pin cushion	tinta	**14.** paint
linha	**4.** thread	**escultura**	**I. sculpting/sculpture**
agulha	**5.** (sewing) needle	massa/gesso	**15.** plaster
dedal	**6.** thimble	pedra	**16.** stone
pano/fazenda	**7.** material	**cerâmica**	**J. pottery**
tricô	**B. knitting**	argila	**17.** clay
agulha de tricô	**8.** knitting needle	torno (de oleiro)	**18.** potter's wheel
lã	**9.** yarn	**carpintaria**	**K. woodworking**
tecer	**C. weaving**	**coleção de selos**	**L. stamp collecting**
tear	**10.** loom	álbum de selos	**19.** stamp album
crochê	**D. crocheting**	**colecionar moedas**	**M. coin collecting**
agulha de crochê	**11.** crochet hook	catálogo de moedas	**20.** coin catalog
bordado em tela	**E. needlepoint**	álbum de moedas	**21.** coin album
bordado em tecido	**F. embroidery**	**modelismo**	**N. model building**
fazer acolchoados	**G. quilting**	kit de modelismo	**22.** model kit

cola de modelismo	**23.** (model) glue
tinta de modelismo	**24.** (model) paint
ornitologia	**O. bird watching**
binóculo	**25.** binoculars
guia	**26.** field guide
fotografia	**P. photography**
máquina fotográfica	**27.** camera
astronomia	**Q. astronomy**
telescópio	**28.** telescope
jogos	**R. games**
xadrez	**29.** chess
damas	**30.** checkers
gamão	**31.** backgammon
Banco Imobiliário	**32.** Monopoly
palavras cruzadas	**33.** Scrabble
cartas/baralho	**34.** cards
Master	**35.** Trivial Pursuit
bolas de gude	**36.** marbles
jogo de pinos	**37.** jacks

[1–28]   [In a store]
  A. May I help you?
  B. Yes, please. I'd like to buy
    (a/an) _____.

[29–37]   [At home]
  A. What do you want to do?
  B. Let's play _____.

What's your hobby?
What games are popular in your
  country? Describe how to play one.

ENTRETENIMENTOS

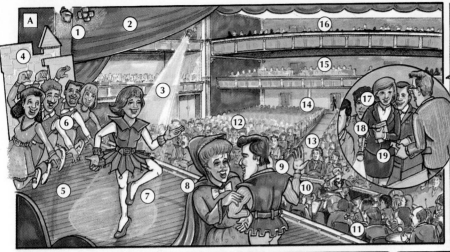

teatro	**A. theater**		balcão	**15.** mezzanine	balé	**D. ballet**
luzes	**1.** lights/lighting		galeria	**16.** balcony	bailarino	**27.** ballet dancer
cortina/pano	**2.** curtain		lanterninha	**17.** usher	bailarina	**28.** ballerina
holofote	**3.** spotlight		programa	**18.** program	companhia de balé	**29.** ballet company
cenário	**4.** scenery		bilhete/entrada/ingresso	**19.** ticket	sapatilhas	**30.** ballet slippers
palco	**5.** stage				sapatilha de ponta	**31.** toeshoes
coro	**6.** chorus		sinfonia	**B. symphony**		
bailarina/bailarino	**7.** dancer		orquestra sinfônica	**20.** symphony orchestra	cinema	**E. movies**
atriz	**8.** actress		músico	**21.** musician	marquise	**32.** marquee
ator	**9.** actor		regente	**22.** conductor	bilheteria	**33.** box office
orquestra	**10.** orchestra		batuta	**23.** baton	cartaz	**34.** billboard
(local da) orquestra	**11.** orchestra pit		pódio	**24.** podium	saguão	**35.** lobby
platéia/espectadores	**12.** audience				bar	**36.** refreshment
corredor	**13.** aisle		ópera	**C. opera**		stand
orquestra	**14.** orchestra		cantor/cantora de ópera	**25.** opera singer	tela	**37.** (movie) screen
			companhia de ópera	**26.** opera company		

[A–E]
A. What are you doing this evening?
B. I'm going to the _____.

[1–11, 20–37]
A. { What a magnificent _____!
    { What magnificent _____s!
B. I agree.

[14–16]
A. Where did you sit during
   the performance?
B. We sat in the _____.

What kinds of entertainment on this page are popular in your country?

Tell about a play, concert, opera, ballet, or movie you have seen. Describe the performance and the theater.

música	A. music	peças teatrais	B. plays	programas de TV	D. TV programs
música clássica	1. classical music	drama	13. drama	drama	24. drama
música popular	2. popular music	comédia	14. comedy	comédia (seriado)	25. (situation) comedy/
música country	3. country music	musical (comédia)	15. musical (comedy)		sitcom
rock	4. rock music			talk show	26. talk show
música folclórica	5. folk music	filmes	C. movies	programa de	27. game show
rap	6. rap music	drama	16. drama	auditório/jogos	
gospel	7. gospel music	comédia	17. comedy	noticiário	28. news program
jazz	8. jazz	foroeste	18. western	programa de esportes	29. sports program
blues	9. blues	desenho animado	19. cartoon	programa infantil	30. children's program
música sertaneja	10. bluegrass	filme estrangeiro	20. foreign film	desenho animado	31. cartoon
heavy metal	11. heavy metal	filme de aventura	21. adventure movie		
reggae	12. reggae	filme de guerra	22. war movie		
		filme de ficção	23. science fiction		
		científica	movie		

A. What kind of __[A–D]__ do you like?

B. { I like __[1–12]__ .
{ I like __[13–31]__ s.

What's your favorite type of music?	What kind of movies do you like?	What kind of TV programs do you like?
Who is your favorite singer? musician?	Who are your favorite movie stars?	What are your favorite shows?
musical group?	What are the titles of your favorite	
	movies?	

INSTRUMENTOS MUSICAIS

A. Do you play a musical instrument?
B. Yes. I play the **violin**.

Cordas	**A. Strings**				
violino	**1.** violin	clarineta	**13.** clarinet	conga/tambor alto	**25.** conga (drum)
viola	**2.** viola	oboé	**14.** oboe	pratos	**26.** cymbals
violãocelo	**3.** cello	flauta a bico	**15.** recorder	xilofone	**27.** xylophone
contrabaixo	**4.** bass	saxofone	**16.** saxophone		
violão/guitarra	**5.** (acoustic) guitar	fagote	**17.** bassoon	Teclados	**E. Keyboard**
ukelele/guitarra	**6.** ukelele				**Instruments**
havaiana		Metais	**C. Brass**	piano	**28.** piano
guitarra elétrica	**7.** electric guitar	trombeta/clarim	**18.** trumpet	órgão	**29.** organ
banjo	**8.** banjo	trombone	**19.** trombone	teclado eletrônico	**30.** electric piano/
bandolim	**9.** mandolin	trompa	**20.** French horn		digital piano
harpa	**10.** harp	contrabaixo/	**21.** tuba	sintetizador	**31.** synthesizer
		trombone			
		Percussão	**D. Percussion**	Outros Instrumentos	**F. Other Instruments**
Sopro	**B. Woodwinds**	tambor	**22.** drum	acordeão/sanfona	**32.** accordion
flautim	**11.** piccolo	timbale/tímpano	**23.** kettle drum	gaita	**33.** harmonica
flauta	**12.** flute	bongo/tambor duplo	**24.** bongos		

A. You play the _____ very well.
B. Thank you.

A. What's that noise?
B. That's my son/daughter practicing the _____.

Do you play a musical instrument?
   Which one?
Name and describe other musical instruments used in your country.

árvore	**1.** tree	bordo	**18.** maple	gardênia	**34.** gardenia
folha–folhas	**2.** leaf–leaves	carvalho	**19.** oak	lírio	**35.** lily
galho pequeno	**3.** twig	pinheiro	**20.** pine	amor-perfeito	**36.** pansy
galho	**4.** branch	sequóia	**21.** redwood	petúnia	**37.** petunia
ramo	**5.** limb	chorão/salgueiro	**22.** (weeping) willow	orquídea	**38.** orchid
tronco	**6.** trunk	flor	**23.** flower	rosa	**39.** rose
casca	**7.** bark	pétala	**24.** petal	girassol	**40.** sunflower
raiz	**8.** root	pistilo	**25.** pistula	tulipa	**41.** tulip
agulha	**9.** needle	estame	**26.** stamen	violeta	**42.** violet
pinha/cone	**10.** cone	caule	**27.** stem	moita	**43.** bush
corniso	**11.** dogwood	botão	**28.** bud	arbusto	**44.** shrub
azevinho	**12.** holly	espinho	**29.** thorn	samambaia	**45.** fern
magnólia	**13.** magnolia	bulbo	**30.** bulb	planta	**46.** plant
olmo	**14.** elm	crislântemo	**31.** chrysanthemum/	cacto–cactos	**47.** cactus–cacti
cerejeira	**15.** cherry		mum	videira	**48.** vine
palmeira	**16.** palm	narciso	**32.** daffodil	grama	**49.** grass
vidoeiro	**17.** birch	margarida	**33.** daisy	toxicodendro	**50.** poison ivy

[11–22]
A. What kind of tree is that?
B. I think it's a/an _____ tree.

[31–48]
A. Look at all the _____s!
B. They're beautiful!

Describe your favorite tree and your favorite flower.
What kinds of trees and flowers grow where you live?

In your country, are flowers used at weddings? at funerals?
on holidays? on visits to the hospital? Tell which flowers are
used for different occasions.

O MEIO AMBIENTE E AS FONTES DE ENERGIA

floresta/mata	**1.** forest/woods	penhasco	**13.** cliff
lago	**2.** lake	desfiladeiro/garganta	**14.** canyon
pradaria	**3.** meadow	rio	**15.** river
montanha	**4.** mountain	barragem	**16.** dam
vale	**5.** valley	deserto	**17.** desert
cachoeira/catarata	**6.** waterfall	duna/banco de areia	**18.** dune
rápidos	**7.** rapids	selva	**19.** jungle
colina/encosta	**8.** hill	costa/litoral/praia	**20.** seashore
campo	**9.** field	baía	**21.** bay
riacho/córrego	**10.** stream/brook	oceano	**22.** ocean
lago pequeno	**11.** pond	ilha	**23.** island
planalto	**12.** plateau	poluição do ar	**24.** air pollution

chuva ácida	**25.** acid rain
lixo tóxico	**26.** toxic waste
radiação	**27.** radiation
poluição da água	**28.** water pollution
petróleo	**29.** oil
gás (natural)	**30.** (natural) gas
carvão	**31.** coal
vento	**32.** wind
energia nuclear	**33.** nuclear energy
energia solar	**34.** solar energy
energia hidroelétrica	**35.** hydroelectric power

[1–23]　A.　{ Isn't this a beautiful _____?!
　　　　　　{ Aren't these beautiful _____?!
　　　　B.　It's/They're magnificent.

[24–28]　A.　Do you worry about the environment?
　　　　　B.　Yes.　I'm very concerned about _____.

Describe some places of natural beauty in your country.

What kind of energy do you use to heat your home? to cook?
In your opinion, which kind of energy is best for producing electricity?

casa de fazenda	**1.** farmhouse	colheitadeira	**14.** combine	peru	**27.** turkey
horta	**2.** (vegetable) garden	pasto	**15.** pasture	cabra	**28.** goat
espantalho	**3.** scarecrow	pomar	**16.** orchard	cabrito	**29.** kid
plantação	**4.** crop	árvore frutífera	**17.** fruit tree	carneiro/ovelha	**30.** sheep
sistema de irrigação	**5.** irrigation system	fazendeiro	**18.** farmer	cordeiro	**31.** lamb
celeiro	**6.** barn	empregado	**19.** hired hand	touro	**32.** bull
silo	**7.** silo	cercado para galinhas	**20.** chicken coop	vaca (leiteira)	**33.** (dairy) cow
estábulo	**8.** stable	galinheiro	**21.** hen house	bezerro-bezerros	**34.** calf–calves
feno	**9.** hay	cerca	**22.** fence	cavalo	**35.** horse
forcado	**10.** pitchfork	trator	**23.** tractor	porco	**36.** pig
cercado/terreiro	**11.** barnyard	galo	**24.** rooster	leitão	**37.** piglet
chiqueiro	**12.** pig pen/pig sty	galinha	**25.** chicken/hen		
campo	**13.** field	pinto	**26.** chick		

A. Where's the _____?
B. In/On/Next to the _____.

A. The _[24–37]_ s got loose again!
B. Oh, no! Where are they?
A. They're in the _[1, 2, 12, 13, 15, 16, 20, 21]_ !

Tell about farms in your country.
What crops and animals are common on these farms?

ANIMAIS E BICHOS DE ESTIMAÇÃO

raposa	**1.** fox	castor	**14.** beaver	leopardo	**27.** leopard
porco-espinho	**2.** porcupine	morcego	**15.** bat	pintas	**a.** spots
espinho	**a.** quill	gambá	**16.** skunk	girafa	**28.** giraffe
racum	**3.** raccoon	jaritaca	**17.** possum	bisão	**29.** bison
lobo(s)	**4.** wolf–wolves	burro	**18.** donkey	elefante	**30.** elephant
alce	**5.** moose	búfalo	**19.** buffalo	presa	**a.** tusk
chifre	**a.** antler	camelo	**20.** camel	tromba	**b.** trunk
veado	**6.** deer	corcunda	**a.** hump	tigre	**31.** tiger
casco/pata	**a.** hoof	lhama	**21.** llama	pata	**a.** paw
veado pequeno	**7.** fawn	cavalo	**22.** horse	leão	**32.** lion
camundongo(s)	**8.** mouse–mice	rabo	**a.** tail	juba	**a.** mane
tâmia/esquilo	**9.** chipmunk	potro	**23.** foal	hipopótamo	**33.** hippopotamus
listrado		pônei	**24.** pony	hiena	**34.** hyena
rato	**10.** rat	tatu	**25.** armadillo	rinoceronte	**35.** rhinoceros
esquilo	**11.** squirrel	cangaru	**26.** kangaroo	chifre	**a.** horn
coelho	**12.** rabbit	bolsa	**a.** pouch	zebra	**36.** zebra
geômio	**13.** gopher			listras	**a.** stripes

						Bichos de estimação	**Pets**
urso preto	**37.** black bear		gibão	**44.** gibbon		gato	**51.** cat
garra	**a.** claw		babuíno	**45.** baboon		bigode	**a.** whiskers
urso americano	**38.** grizzly bear		orangotango	**46.** orangutan		gatinho	**52.** kitten
urso polar	**39.** polar bear		gorila	**47.** gorilla		cão/cachorro	**53.** dog
urso coala	**40.** koala (bear)		tamanduá	**48.** anteater		cachorrinho/filhote	**54.** puppy
panda	**41.** panda		minhoca	**49.** worm		hâmster	**55.** hamster
macaco	**42.** monkey		lesma	**50.** slug		gerbo	**56.** gerbil
chimpanzé	**43.** chimpanzee					porquinho da Índia	**57.** guinea pig

[1–50] A. Look at that _____!
B. Wow! That's the biggest _____ I've ever seen!

[51–57] A. Do you have a pet?
B. Yes. I have a _____.
A. What's your _____'s name?
B. …………

What animals can be found where you live?
Is there a zoo near where you live? What animals does the zoo have?
What are some common pets in your country?

If you were an animal, which animal do you think you would be? Why?
Does your culture have any popular folk tales or children's stories about animals? Tell a story you are familiar with.

Pássaros	A. **Birds**		coruja	**12.** owl		pinguim	**28.** penguin		abelha	**41.** bee
tordo americano	**1.** robin		falcão	**13.** hawk		roadrunner	**29.** roadrunner		colméia	**a.** beehive
ninho	**a.** nest		águia	**14.** eagle		(espécie de anum)			lagarta	**42.** caterpillar
ovo	**b.** egg		garra	**a.** claw		avestruz	**30.** ostrich		casulo	**a.** cocoon
gaio	**2.** blue jay		canário	**15.** canary					borboleta	**43.** butterfly
asa	**a.** wing		cacatua	**16.** cockatoo		Insetos	B. **Insects**		gafanhoto	**44.** grasshopper
cauda	**b.** tail		papagaio	**17.** parrot		mosca	**31.** fly		formiga	**45.** ant
pena	**c.** feather		periquito	**18.** parakeet		mosquito/pernilongo	**32.** mosquito		besouro	**46.** beetle
cardinal	**3.** cardinal		pato	**19.** duck		pulga	**33.** flea		cupim	**47.** termite
beija-flor	**4.** hummingbird		bico	**a.** bill		vagalume	**34.** firefly/		barata	**48.** roach/
faisão	**5.** pheasant		patinho	**20.** duckling			lightning bug			cockroach
corvo	**6.** crow		ganso	**21.** goose		mariposa	**35.** moth		escorpião	**49.** scorpion
gaivota	**7.** seagull		cisne	**22.** swan		libélula	**36.** dragonfly		centopéia	**50.** centipede
pardal	**8.** sparrow		flamingo	**23.** flamingo		aranha	**37.** spider		louva-deus	**51.** praying
pica-pau	**9.** woodpecker		garça	**24.** crane		teia	**a.** web			mantis
bico	**a.** beak		cegonha	**25.** stork		joaninha	**38.** ladybug		grilo	**52.** cricket
andorinha	**10.** swallow		pelicano	**26.** pelican		vespa	**39.** wasp			
pombo	**11.** pigeon		pavão	**27.** peacock		carrapato	**40.** tick			

[1–52] A. Is that a/an _____?
B. No. I think it's a/an _____.

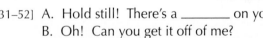

[31–52] A. Hold still! There's a _____ on your shirt!
B. Oh! Can you get it off of me?
A. There! It's gone!

What birds and insects can be found where you live?

Does your culture have any popular folk tales or children's stories about birds or insects? Tell a story you are familiar with.

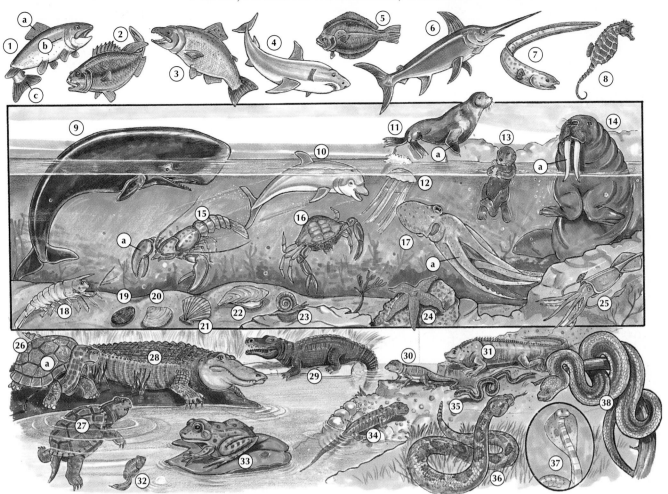

Peixes	**A. Fish**
truta	**1.** trout
barbatana/asa	**a.** fin
guelra	**b.** gill
cauda	**c.** tail
perca	**2.** bass
salmão	**3.** salmon
tubarão	**4.** shark
linguado	**5.** flounder
peixe-espada	**6.** swordfish
enguia	**7.** eel
cavalo-marinho	**8.** sea horse

Animais Marinhos	**B. Sea Animals**
baleia	**9.** whale
golfinho	**10.** dolphin
foca	**11.** seal
nadadeira	**a.** flipper

água-viva	**12.** jellyfish
lontra	**13.** otter
leão marinho	**14.** walrus
dente/presa	**a.** tusk
lagosta	**15.** lobster
garra	**a.** claw
caranguejo	**16.** crab
polvo	**17.** octopus
tentáculo	**a.** tentacle
camarão	**18.** shrimp
mexilhão	**19.** mussel
marisco	**20.** clam
vieira	**21.** scallop
ostra	**22.** oyster
caracol	**23.** snail
estrela-do-mar	**24.** starfish
lula	**25.** squid

Anfíbios e Répteis	**C. Amphibians and Reptiles**
tartaruga	**26.** tortoise
casca	**a.** shell
cágado	**27.** turtle
jacaré	**28.** alligator
crocodilo	**29.** crocodile
lagartixa	**30.** lizard
iguana	**31.** iguana
girino	**32.** tadpole
sapo/rã	**33.** frog
salamandra	**34.** salamander
cobra	**35.** snake
cascavél	**36.** rattlesnake
naja	**37.** cobra
jibóia	**38.** boa constrictor

[1–38] A. Is that a/an _____?
B. No. I think it's a/an _____.

[26–38] A. Are there any _____s around here?
B. No. But there are lots of _____s.

What fish, sea animals, and reptiles can be found in your country? Which ones are endangered and need to be protected? Why?

In your opinion, which ones are the most interesting? the most beautiful? the most dangerous?

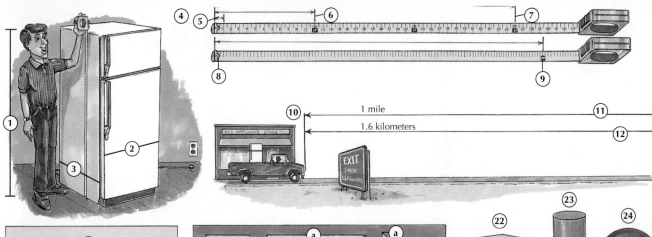

1 mile
1.6 kilometers

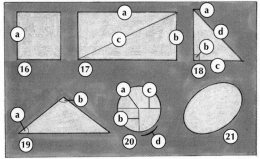

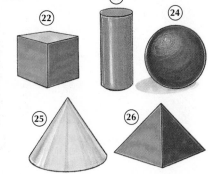

Medidas	**A. Measurements**	linhas paralelas	**14.** parallel lines	triângulo isóscele	**19.** isosceles triangle
altura	**1.** height	linhas perpendiculares	**15.** perpendicular	ângulo agudo	**a.** acute angle
largura	**2.** width		lines	ângulo obtuso	**b.** obtuse angle
profundidade	**3.** depth			círculo	**20.** circle
comprimento	**4.** length	**Formas Geométricas**	**C. Geometric Shapes**	centro	**a.** center
polegada	**5.** inch	quadrado	**16.** square	raio	**b.** radius
pé-pés	**6.** foot–feet	lado	**a.** side	diâmetro	**c.** diameter
jarda	**7.** yard	retângulo	**17.** rectangle	circunferência	**d.** circumference
centímetro	**8.** centimeter	comprimento	**a.** length	elipse/oval	**21.** ellipse/oval
metro	**9.** meter	largura	**b.** width		
distância	**10.** distance	diagonal	**c.** diagonal	**Figuras Sólidas**	**D. Solid Figures**
milha	**11.** mile	triângulo retângulo	**18.** right triangle	cubo	**22.** cube
quilômetro	**12.** kilometer	ápice	**a.** apex	cilindro	**23.** cylinder
		ângulo reto	**b.** right angle	esfera	**24.** sphere
Linhas	**B. Lines**	base	**c.** base	cone	**25.** cone
linha reta	**13.** straight line	hipotenusa	**d.** hypotenuse	pirâmide	**26.** pyramid

[1–9]
A. What's the __[1–4]__ ?
B. .... __[5–9]__ (s).

[11–12]
A. What's the distance?
B. .... _____(s).

1 inch (1")	=	2.54 centimeters (cm)
1 foot (1')	=	0.305 meters (m)
1 yard (1 yd.)	=	0.914 meters (m)
1 mile (mi.)	=	1.6 kilometers (km)

[16–21]
A. Who can tell me what shape this is?
B. I can. It's a/an _____.

[22–26]
A. Who knows what figure this is?
B. I do. It's a/an _____.

[13–26]
A. This painting is magnificent!
B. Hmm. I don't think so. It just looks like a lot of _____s and _____s to me!

O UNIVERSO E A EXPLORAÇÃO DO ESPAÇO SIDERAL

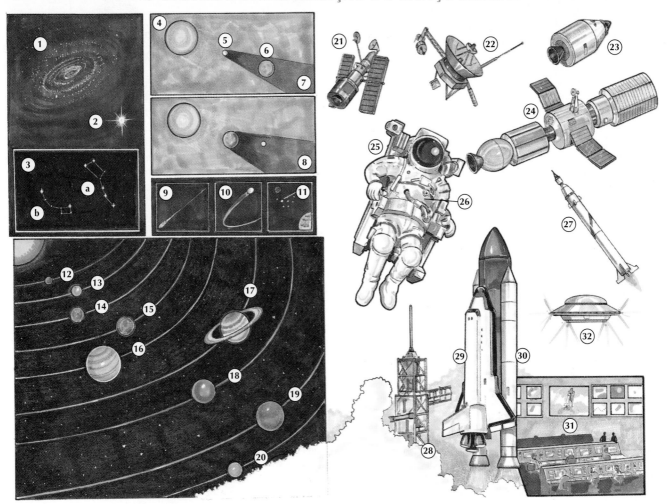

O Universo	**A. The Universe**	cometa	**10.** comet	sonda espacial	**22.** (space) probe
galáxia	**1.** galaxy	asteróide	**11.** asteroid	nave espacial	**23.** space craft/orbiter
estrela	**2.** star	Mercúrio	**12.** Mercury	estação espacial	**24.** space station
constelação	**3.** constellation	Vênus	**13.** Venus	astronauta	**25.** astronaut
Ursa Maior	**a.** The Big Dipper	Terra	**14.** Earth	roupa espacial	**26.** space suit
Ursa Menor	**b.** The Little Dipper	Marte	**15.** Mars	foguete	**27.** rocket
		Júpiter	**16.** Jupiter	plataforma de	**28.** launch pad
O Sistema Solar	**B. The Solar System**	Saturno	**17.** Saturn	lançamento	
sol	**4.** sun	Urano	**18.** Uranus	ônibus espacial	**29.** space shuttle
lua	**5.** moon	Netuno	**19.** Neptune	foguete auxiliar	**30.** booster rocket
planeta	**6.** planet	Plutão	**20.** Pluto	estação de controle	**31.** mission control
eclipse	**7.** solar eclipse			OVNI/ Objeto	**32.** U.F.O./
eclipse lunar	**8.** lunar eclipse	**Exploração do**	**C. Space Exploration**	Voador Não	Unidentified
meteoro	**9.** meteor	**Espaço Sideral**		Identificado/	Flying Object/
		satélite	**21.** satellite	disco voador	flying saucer

[1–20]

A. Is that (a/an/the) _____?

B. I'm not sure. I think it might be (a/an/the) _____.

[21–27, 29, 31]

A. Is the _____ ready for tomorrow's launch?

B. Yes. "All systems are go!"

Pretend you are an astronaut traveling in space.
What do you see?
Draw and name a constellation you are familiar with.

Do you think space exploration is important? Why?
Have you ever seen a U.F.O.? Do you believe there is
life in outer space? Why?

GLOSSÁRIO

O número em negrito indica a página (páginas) onde a palavra correspondente em inglês aparece; o número seguinte indica a localização da palavra em inglês na ilustração e na lista de palavras naquela página. Por exemplo, 'norte 5-1' indica que a palavra em inglês que significa norte está localizada na página 5 e seu número na lista é 1

GLOSSARY

The bold number indicates the page(s) on which the word appears; the number that follows indicates the word's location in the illustration and in the word list on the page. For example, "north **5**-1" indicates that the word *north* is on page 5 and is item number 1.

a.m. **32**
abdomen **68**-30
accelerator **93**-70
accessories **60**
accordion **112**-32
accountant **80**-1
acid rain **114**-25
acorn squash **45**-11
acoustic guitar **112**-5
act **84**-1
action figure **65**-14
actor **80**-2, **110**-9
actress **80**-3, **110**-8
acute angle **120**-19a
adapter **64**-29
add **53**-12
adding machine **64**-27, **87**-9
addition **31**
address **1**-5, **75**-19
adhesive tape **72**-25
administrative assistant **86**-30
adventure movie **111**-21
aerogramme **75**-3
afraid **43**-26
Africa **6**-4
after shave lotion **23**-25
ailment **70**
air bag **93**-59
air conditioner **26**-11
air conditioning **93**-64
air filter **92**-32
air freshener **22**-5
air letter **75**-3
air mail **75**-6
air mattress **101**-22
air pollution **114**-24
air pump **92**-40
air sickness bag **97**-30
air tank **107**-18
airplane **97**-35
airport **96**
aisle **49**-71, **97**-14, **110**-13
aisle seat **97**-18
alarm clock **17**-15
alcohol **72**-26
algebra **78**-2
alligator **119**-28
alternator **92**-35
aluminum foil **49**-61
American..**12**
American cheese **48**-7
ammonia **24**-25
amphibian **119**-C
amplifier **63**-10
anesthetic **72**-29
angry **43**-19
animal **116**
ankle **69**-54
annoyed **43**-17

answer **11**-13, 23
answering machine **64**-14
ant **118**-45
antacid tablets **74**-7
Antarctica **6**-8
anteater **117**-48
antenna **92**-11
antipasto (plate) **55**-10
antler **116**-5a
apartment **13**-1
apartment building **13**-1
apartment number **1**-8
apex **120**-18a
appetizer **55**
apple **44**-1
apple juice **46**-26
apple pie **55**-26
appliance repair person **27**-5
appliance store **34**-1
appointment book **88**-22
apricot **44**-6
archery **103**-V
architect **80**-4
area code **1**-12
arm **68**-32
armadillo **116**-25
armchair **14**-4
armpit **68**-33
armrest **93**-79, **97**-24
arrival and departure board **95**-3
arrival and departure monitor **96**-4
art **78**-20
arteries **69**-79
artichoke **45**-24
artist **80**-5
ashamed **43**-30
Asia **6**-6
asparagus **45**-8
aspirin **74**-1
assemble **84**-2
assembler **80**-6
assembly line **90**-6
assistant principal **77**-18
asteroid **121**-11
astronaut **121**-25
astronomy **109**-Q
athletic supporter **58**-9
atlas **76**-13
ATM (machine) **67**-17
ATM card **67**-7
attendant **92**-43
audience **110**-12
audio cassette **63**-17
audio tape **63**-17
auditorium **77**-13
aunt **3**-1
Australia **6**-7

author **76**-27
auto dealer **34**-2
automatic teller (machine) **67**-17
automatic transmission **93**-72
autumn **98**-27
avocado **44**-13

baboon **117**-45
baby **2**-9
baby carriage **20**-23
baby carrier **20**-29
baby cereal **49**-64
baby food **21**-6, **49**-66
baby lotion **21**-2
baby powder **21**-1
baby products **49**-I
baby seat **20**-26
baby shampoo **21**-3
baby wipes **21**-7
baby's room **20**
back **68**-31
back door **25**-22
backache **70**-5
backboard **105**-22
backgammon **109**-31
backhoe **91**-23
backpack **60**-23, **99**-2
backup light **92**-19
bacon **47**-56
bacon, lettuce, and tomato sandwich **54**-28
bad **40**-32
bag **50**-1
bagel **54**-3
baggage **95**-11, **96**-21
baggage carousel **96**-17
baggage claim (area) **96**-16
baggage claim check **96**-23
baggage compartment **95**-19
bagger **49**-83
baggy **61**-4
bait **107**-29
bake **53**-17, **84**-3
baked chicken **55**-16
baked goods **47**-I
baked potato **55**-19
baker **80**-7
bakery **34**-3
baking products **48**-E
balance beam **103**-41
balcony **26**-19, **110**-16
ballerina **110**-28
ballet **110**-D
ballet company **110**-29
ballet dancer **110**-27
ballet slippers **110**-30
ballfield **104**-2, 4
banana **44**-4

band **79**-22
band shell **100**-12
bandages **72**-24
bandaid **73**-3
banjo **112**-8
bank **34**-4, **67**
bank book **67**-4
bank officer **67**-18
bank vault **67**-13
bar **50**-2
barbecue **25**-29, **53**-23
barbell **103**-46
barber **80**-8
barber shop **34**-5
bark **113**-7
barn **115**-6
barnyard **115**-11
barrettes **23**-17
barrier **94**-8
base **23**-33, **120**-18c
baseball **104**-A, **105**-1
baseball cap **59**-29
baseball field **104**-2
baseball glove **105**-6
baseball player **104**-1
baseball uniform **105**-4
basketball **104**-F, **105**-21
basketball court **104**-12
basketball hoop **105**-23
basketball player **104**-11
bass **112**-4
bass **119**-2
bassoon **112**-17
bat **105**-2, **116**-15
bath mat **22**-41
bath rug **22**-41
bath towel **22**-10
bathing cap **101**-18, **107**-13
bathing suit **101**-17, **107**-11
bathrobe **58**-4
bathroom **22**, **97**-10
bathroom scale **22**-14
bathroom sink **22**-20
bathtub **22**-37
baton **110**-23
batteries **29**-25
battery **92**-33
batting helmet **105**-3
bay **114**-21
beach **101**
beach ball **65**-6, **101**-30
beach blanket **101**-24
beach chair **101**-15
beach towel **101**-16
beach umbrella **101**-14
beads **60**-8
beak **118**-9a
beam **91**-32
beard **68**-26

long **40**-3, **61**-1
long johns **58**-10
long underwear **58**-10
long-sleeved shirt **57**-1
loom **109**-10
loose **40**-13, **61**-4
lotion **74**-12
loud **40**-45
loudspeaker **10**-22
loveseat **14**-19
low **40**-8, **61**-8
low-fat milk **46**-2
lower *the shades* **11**-26
luggage **95**-11
luggage carrier **92**-13, **96**-19
luggage compartment **95**-19
luggage rack **92**-13
lumber **91**-25
lunar eclipse **121**-8
lunch **8**-17
lunchroom monitor **77**-21
lungs **69**-66

macaroni **46**-24
macaroni salad **48**-14
machine **90**-11
mad **43**-19
magazine **49**-86, **76**-23
magnolia **113**-13
mail bag **75**-32
mail carrier **75**-31
mail slot **75**-24
mail truck **75**-29
mailbox **25**-2, **26**-4, **75**-30,
  86-5
mailer **89**-20
mailing label **89**-21
mailroom **86**-14
make breakfast **8**-16
make dinner **8**-18
make lunch **8**-17
make the bed **8**-11
makeup **23**
mall **37**-22
mandolin **112**-9
mane **116**-32a
mango **44**-10
manhole **38**-11
manila folder **89**-16
mantel **14**-23
manual transmission **93**-75
map **10**-25
maple **113**-18
marbles **109**-36
margarine **46**-9
markers **65**-23
marmalade **49**-48
marquee **110**-32
married **40**-47
Mars **121**-15
mascara **23**-38
mashed potatoes **55**-20

mask **90**-5, **107**-14,19
masking tape **89**-26
mason **80**-10
mat **103**-43, 53
matchbox car **65**-16
material **109**-7
maternity shop **36**-6
math **78**-1
mathematics **31**, **78**-1
mattress **17**-22
mayonnaise **48**-33
meadow **114**-3
meal **97**-27
measurement **120**-A
measuring cup **19**-17
measuring spoon **19**-18
meat **47**-G
meatloaf **55**-13
mechanic **82**-2, **92**-42
mechanical pencil **88**-34
media section **76**-16
median **94**-13
medical chart **73**-26
medicine **74**
medicine cabinet **22**-19
medicine chest **22**-19
memo holder **88**-6
memo pad **89**-12
Men's Clothing Department
  62-3
men's room **62**-7
Mercury **121**-12
merry-go-round **100**-8
message board **86**-4
message pad **89**-14
messenger **81**-18
messy **40**-42
metal detector **96**-8
meteor **121**-9
meter **95**-38, **120**-9
meter maid **38**-18
mezzanine **110**-15
microcassette recorder **87**-10
microfiche **76**-5
microfilm **76**-4
microwave **53**-25
microwave (oven) **18**-15
Middle East **6**-5
middle finger **69**-47
middle lane **94**-15
middle name **1**-3
middle seat **97**-17
midnight **32**
mile **120**-11
milk **46**-1, **54**-21
minivan **93**-88
minus **31**
mirror **17**-18, **22**-18
miserable **42**-13
mission control **121**-31
mistake **11**-19
mittens **59**-26

mix **53**-15
mixed vegetables **55**-24
mixer **19**-23
mixing bowl **19**-15
mobile **20**-6
mobile home **13**-7
moccasins **58**-36
model **82**-3
model building **109**-N
model glue **109**-23
model kit **65**-20, **109**-22
model paint **109**-24
modeling clay **65**-27
modem **64**-7
money **66**
money order **67**-11, **75**-15
monitor **64**-2
monkey **117**-42
monkey bars **100**-20
monkey wrench **28**-8
Monopoly **109**-32
month **33**
monthly statement **67**-3
moon **121**-5
moose **116**-5
mop **24**-13,14,15
mortgage payment **27**-21
mosquito **118**-32
motel **36**-7
moth **118**-35
mother **2**-3
mother-in-law **3**-6
mountain **114**-4
mountain climbing **99**-C
mouse **64**-5, **116**-8
mousetrap **29**-24
mouth **68**-19
mouthwash **23**-22
movie **111**-C
movie projector **10**-34
movie screen **10**-31, **64**-23,
  110-37
movie theater **36**-8
movies **110**-E
mow **85**-15
mozzarella **48**-10
muffin **54**-2
muffler **92**-22
muggy **98**-7
multiplication **31**
mum **113**-31
muscles **69**-73
museum **36**-9
mushroom **45**-23
music **78**-21, **111**-A
music store **36**-10
musical (comedy) **111**-15
musical instrument **112**
musician **110**-21
mussel **47**-66, **119**-19
mustache **68**-25
mustard **48**-25

nacho chips **48**-19
nachos **55**-5
nail **28**-28
nail brush **23**-12
nail clipper **23**-11
nail file **23**-9
nail polish **23**-31
nail polish remover **23**-32
name **1**-1
nameplate **88**-9
napkin **16**-9, **49**-51
narrow **40**-22, **61**-16
nasal spray **74**-8
nationality **12**
natural gas **114**-30
nauseous **71**-29
navy blue **56**-15
neat **40**-41
neck **68**-27
necklace **60**-5
necktie **57**-27
nectarine **44**-7
needle **72**-23, **109**-5, **113**-9
needlepoint **109**-E
neon green **56**-18
nephew **3**-4
Neptune **121**-19
nervous **43**-24
nest **118**-1a
net **102**-31, **107**-28
new **40**-27
news program **111**-28
newscaster **82**-4
newspaper **76**-22
newsstand **39**-37
nickel **66**
niece **3**-3
night club **36**-11
night light **20**-8
night table **17**-14
nightgown **58**-2
nightshirt **58**-3
nightstand **17**-14
nipple **21**-15
no left turn sign **94**-34
no right turn sign **94**-35
No Smoking sign **97**-20
no U-turn sign **94**-36
noisy **40**-45
noodles **46**-23, **55**-23
noon **32**
north **5**-1
North America **6**-1
northeast **5**-5
northwest **5**-6
nose **68**-15, **97**-36
nostril **68**-16
note pad **89**-12
notebook **10**-11
notebook computer **64**-11
notebook paper **10**-12
notes **11**-30

ÍNDICE TEMÁTICO